NEW YORK REVIEW BOOKS

POETS

EUGENIO MONTALE (1896–1981) was born in Genoa. In his teens, he studied accounting at vocational school and pursued his passion for poetry largely alone at the library. After serving in the infantry in the Great War and training to be an opera singer, he published his debut collection, *Cuttlefish Bones*, in 1925 — the first of many books of poetry that would establish him as the leading Italian writer of his generation. A sworn anti-Fascist, he spent most of the Mussolini era barely making ends meet in Florence, where he got to know, among others, Carlo Emilio Gadda, Tommaso Landolfi, and Irma Brandeis (the subject of some of his most ardent love poems). In 1948, Montale moved to Milan, becoming a regular contributor to the newspaper *Corriere della Sera*, for which he wrote most of the prose pieces that became *Butterfly of Dinard* (published by NYRB Classics). After taking a hiatus from poetry for much of the 1960s, he returned with *Satura* in 1971, followed by several other late works remarkable for their unstudied epigrammatic elegance. He was awarded the Nobel Prize in Literature in 1975.

GEORGE BRADLEY is the author of six books of verse (most recently, *A Stroll in the Rain: New & Selected Poems*, 2021) and the editor of *The Yale Younger Poets Anthology* (1997). The recipient of the Yale Younger Poets Prize and the Witter Bynner Prize from the American Academy of Arts and Letters, among other awards, he has worked variously as a sommelier, an editor, and a copywriter, as well as in construction. Currently he imports and distributes a brand of olive oil from Italy (La Bontà di Fiesole). When not overseas, he lives mostly in Chester, near the river of rivers in Connecticut.

T0034577

Eugenio Montale

Late Montale

SELECTED AND TRANSLATED FROM
THE ITALIAN BY GEORGE BRADLEY

NYRB/POETS

 NEW YORK REVIEW BOOKS   *New York*

THIS IS A NEW YORK REVIEW BOOK
PUBLISHED BY THE NEW YORK REVIEW OF BOOKS
207 East 32nd Street, New York, NY 10016
www.nyrb.com

This selection excerpted from *Eugenio Montale: Tutte le poesie* and *La casa di Olgiate e altre poesie* and first published in 2022 by The Waywiser Press.

A catalog record for this book is available from The Library of Congress.

ISBN 978-1-68137-837-4
Available as an electronic book; ISBN 978-1-68137-838-1

Cover design by Emily Singer

Printed in the United States of America on acid-free paper.
10 9 8 7 6 5 4 3 2 1

Contents

Motifs
Critical Notes
Ruminating

**THE HOUSE IN OLGIATE AND OTHER POEMS
(LA CASA DI OLGIATE E ALTRE POESIE)**

House in Olgiate and Other Poems (*La casa di Olgiate e altre poesie*), that was not published until 2006 and was hence unavailable to previous translators. It is presented here in English in its entirety for the first time. More translations of all of this material will no doubt appear in the future. Montale is so engaging and subtle a poet that his verse will surely continue to inspire attempts to bring it to non-Italian readers worldwide.

The late work has a character of its own. It is that of an older man, soaked in reflection and second thoughts. The poems of the final volumes were composed after the death of the poet's wife in 1963, and thus they are the work of a lonely man, or at least an isolated one, an author whose only companions seem to be his housekeeper and the birds who come to eat the seed he leaves for them on his windowsill. The late poems take as their subject many of Montale's friends and associates, but almost all of these people are dead or otherwise lost. Above all, the verse he wrote toward the end of his life is direct and conversational in a way that his earlier and better known work rarely is. The early poems that made the poet famous are famously enigmatic, highly allusive, and set firmly within the centuries-long tradition of occidental verse. The poems composed in his old age are more straightforward, and if they are ambiguous it is not because they are mysterious in their intentions or hermetic in their meanings, but instead because the author has come to doubt the possibility of any ultimate meaning in itself. The late work is ironic rather than sublime. It is less grand and more intimate, less rhetorical but perhaps more moving, less dazzling yet often more revealing. The poet himself described the difference in an interview: "The first three books were written in a tailcoat, the others in pajamas, or let's say casual clothes." ("*I primi tre libri sono scritti in frac, gli altri in pigiama, o diciamo in abito da passeggio.*") This shift from formality to intimacy and self-revelation parallels the course of twentieth-century poetry as a whole, and similar changes may be seen in the work of many European and American poets. But Montale's achievement seems ever larger with the perspective of passing years, and among those authors whose life work bridged the mid-century compositional watershed, his poetry may yet be deemed the most significant.

In assembling the translations presented here, I have selected poems from three of Montale's final volumes—*Satura, Diary of '71 and '72* (*Diario del '71 e del '72*), and *Four-Year Notebook* (*Quaderno di quattro anni*)—which I find of particular interest and which I think well illustrate aspects of his late work. A fourth—*Other Poems* (*Altri versi*)—I have translated in its entirety, since of all the books published in Montale's lifetime, it has received the least attention. It first appeared as a section of the 1980 *The Work in Verse* (*L'Opera in versi*) rather than as a standalone volume, and following the poet's death a year later it was reissued in combination with his *Fugitive Verse* (*Poesie disperse*). The latter, too, had formed a section of his 1980 volume, where it gathered poems written at various stages of Montale's career which had theretofore been unpublished in book form. Of these, I have translated six. Because it has previously been unavailable in English, I have translated all of *The House in Olgiate and Other Poems*, a collection assembled from material discovered in a university library and published posthumously. There exists another small volume, *Posthumous Diary* (*Diario postumo*), which I have ignored, since it may be found in Jonathan Galassi's accurate rendering, since questions about its authorship persist, and since, as Galassi has said, it shows a notable decline in quality from the rest of the poet's output.

As mentioned, *Other Poems* is not widely celebrated and has received little critical attention. Possibly this is because it has not always been recognized as a book distinct unto itself. Regardless, the book deserves reading. Several of the poems in it ("To a Muse in Training," "Hiding Places II," "Glory or Something Like It") are strong enough to merit inclusion in any selection of the poet's work, and many others are of significant biographical interest. Montale is a muse poet *par excellence*, and the memory of women loved and lost performs a vital function in his poetry. *Other Poems* contains verse addressed to his deceased wife Drusilla Tanzi, as well as a concluding sequence that recalls his brief, youthful acquaintance with Anna degli Uberti. Of particular import is the group of poems having to do with "Clizia," Montale's name for Irma Brandeis. Brandeis was an American scholar living in Florence with whom Montale was involved for much of the 1930s. Among his muses, Clizia is the best known and arguably the most crucial, and the many poems concerning her in this book add to our knowledge of and insight into the poet's complex relationship with her.

The compositions in *The House in Olgiate and Other Poems* were not included by Montale in his 1980 *The Work in Verse*. They are not to be found either in the otherwise definitive *Complete Poems* (*Tutte le poesie*) published retrospectively by Mondadori in 1984, and indeed they could

Montale's later poems are not so dense in literary allusion as his earlier work, but they nonetheless contain a good deal that asks for explication. Even Italian readers, much less foreign ones, are likely to need help with the many people and places the poet mentions in the course of his retrospective ruminations, as well as with his plethora of references to lyric opera. Montale was trained as an operatic bass in his youth—he for a time considered a career as a singer—and his late work is thick with the names of composers, singers, operas and arias. All in all, some help seemed essential, and I have done my best to cast light on the poet's obscurities. That undertaking is easier nowadays than it once was. One may conduct one's research electronically rather than, say, by wandering through a cemetery in Florence or moving to Genoa and buying a street map. To give only one example, the hour-by-hour itinerary of Richard Nixon's state visit to Europe in March of 1969 (apposite to "Nixon in Rome") may now be examined online. The task has also been made easier by the extensive notes provided by Gianfranca Lavezzi to *The House in Olgiate...*, upon which I have relied. In general, though, just as Montale's late work has received relatively little critical attention, it has received less annotation than his earlier poems. William Arrowsmith and Jonathan Galassi, among other translators—as well as Rosanna Bettarini, Gianfranco Contini, and Giorgio Zampa, Montale's Italian editors—have done much to elucidate matters, but questions remain, and I believe the information appended to the poems printed here will clarify at least some of them.

The work of translation always involves difficult choices. There are puns to be approximated, social conventions and cultural mores to be explained to foreign readers, polyvalent words that mean less when uprooted from their native tongue but whose multiple meanings must somehow be conveyed anyway. Anyone seeking to bring poetry out of one language into another will have his or her own philosophy as to how to cope with these challenges and how strictly to adhere to the vocabulary and word-order of the original. When the poetry at hand is so complex and elusive as Montale's, the choices only become more difficult. In general, I have worked to find phrasing and idiom that will seem natural to an English-speaking audience. Montale's late verse does not rhyme regularly, but when it does I have rarely attempted to invent an equivalent. I have also avoided using cognate vocabulary at all costs or following the original word-order regardless of the confusion it might produce, feeling that this would be to abdicate the translator's responsibility and leave too much work to the reader. It is my hope that the versions I have made can stand on their own in English while still retaining some of the flavor of Montale's Italian. I hope, too, that I have been able to convey the essential features of the aged poet's cast of mind: his sardonic self-deprecation; his skepticism regarding grand theories, be they theological, political, or scientific; his Shakespearean conviction that life is a theatrical performance of at best indeterminate import.

No translator should be an island, and I have had help. Geoffrey Brock, Daniel Mark Epstein, Jonathan Galassi, Keith Goldsmith, Richard Howard, Eric Ormsby, Rosanna Warren, and Clive Watkins have been generous with their advice and gracious in their encouragement, and I am most grateful to each of them. I am also grateful to Beatrice Fazio, who has been a highly capable research assistant and a meticulous proofreader of the Italian text. In addition, Philip Hoy has been indefatigable in his attention to this book and has been an enthusiastic collaborator as well as a painstaking editor. Above all, I wish to acknowledge my debt to Professor Riccardo Bruscagli, eminent scholar and valued friend, whose careful reading of these versions and informed suggestions regarding their annotation have been invaluable. He is certainly not responsible for any errors or unwise choices, but I have him to thank for missteps avoided, and it has been a pleasure to partake of his shrewd and sensitive response to Eugenio Montale's profound and fascinating verse.

—GEORGE BRADLEY
Chester, Connecticut

A NOTE ON THE TEXT

Stanza breaks that coincide with page breaks occur at the foot of the following pages: 12, 13, 16, 17, 114, 115, 130, 131, 176, 177, 182, 183, 196, 197.

FROM

Satura (1971)

XENIA I, 13

Tuo fratello morì giovane; tu eri
la bimba scarruffata che mi guarda
'in posa' nell'ovale di un ritratto.
Scrisse musiche inedite, inaudite,
oggi sepolte in un baule o andate
al màcero. Forse le riinventa
qualcuno inconsapevole, se ciò ch'è scritto è scritto.
L'amavo senza averlo mai conosciuto.
Fuori di te nessuno lo ricordava.
Non ho fatto ricerche: ora è inutile.
Dopo di te sono rimasto il solo
per cui egli è esistito. Ma è possibile,
lo sai, amare un'ombra, ombre noi stessi.

XENIA II, 5

Ho sceso, dandoti il braccio, almeno un milione di scale
e ora che non ci sei è il vuoto ad ogni gradino.
Anche così è stato breve il nostro lungo viaggio.
Il mio dura tuttora, né più mi occorrono
le coincidenze, le prenotazioni,
le trappole, gli scorni di chi crede
che la realtà sia quella che si vede.

Ho sceso milioni di scale dandoti il braccio
non già perché con quattr'occhi forse si vede di più.
Con te le ho scese perché sapevo che di noi due
le sole vere pupille, sebbene tanto offuscate,
erano le tue.

XENIA I, 13

Your brother died young. You
were once the disheveled little girl
who strikes a pose and looks at me
out of the oval family portrait.
He wrote music, unpublished, unheard,
buried today in a trunk or left
to rot. Perhaps someone will recreate
his work unwittingly, if what is written is written.
I loved him without knowing him.
Other than you, no one remembered him.
I haven't done any research: there's no point now.
Now that you're gone, I'm the only one left
for whom he ever existed. But it's possible,
you know, to love a shadow, shadows that we are.

XENIA II, 5

Lending you my arm, I went down at least a million
stairs, and now you're gone each step is empty.
All the same, our long journey together was short.
Mine still continues, but I no longer need them,
the connections, the reservations,
the pitfalls, the scorn displayed by those
who believe reality is what they see.

I went down a million stairs with you on my arm
not because four eyes might well see better than two.
I descended them in your company because I knew
that between us, the true eyesight, even if opaque,
was yours.

L'alluvione ha sommerso il pack dei mobili,
delle carte, dei quadri che stipavano
un sotterraneo chiuso a doppio lucchetto.
Forse hanno ciecamente lottato i marocchini
rossi, le sterminate dediche di Du Bos,
il timbro a ceralacca con la barba di Ezra,
il Valéry di Alain, l'originale
dei Canti Orfici – e poi qualche pennello
da barba, mille cianfrusaglie e tutte
le musiche di tuo fratello Silvio.
Dieci, dodici giorni sotto un'atroce morsura
di nafta e sterco. Certo hanno sofferto
tanto prima di perdere la loro identità.
Anch'io sono incrostato fino al collo se il mio
stato civile fu dubbio fin dall'inizio.
Non torba m'ha assediato, ma gli eventi
di una realtà incredibile e mai creduta.
Di fronte ad essi il mio coraggio fu il primo
dei tuoi prestiti e forse non l'hai saputo.

LA STORIA

I.
La storia non si snoda
come una catena
di anelli ininterrotta.
In ogni caso
molti anelli non tengono.
La storia non contiene
il prima e il dopo,
nulla che in lei borbotti
a lento fuoco.
La storia non è prodotta

The flood swamped the clutter of furniture,
of documents, of pictures crammed into
a basement room closed with a double lock.
Maybe they fought blindly, the leather-bound
volumes, the endless dedications of Du Bos,
a wax seal stamped with Ezra's bearded profile,
Alain's commentaries on Valéry, a first edition
of the *Canti Orfici*—plus a few brushes
for shaving, a thousand knick-knacks, and all
the musical compositions of your brother Silvio.
Ten or twelve days under that terrible pressure
of fuel oil and filth—surely they suffered
a lot while they were losing themselves.
I, too, am fighting and in up to my neck, although
my civilian status was dubious from the start.
It isn't dirt that's besieged me, but events
of a reality so incredible I could never believe it.
The courage I faced them with was your greatest
gift to me, and maybe you never knew.

HISTORY

I.
History does not unfold
like a winding chain
of uninterrupted links.
In any case,
many of the links are weak.
History does not contain
a "before" and an "after."
There is nothing in it whispering
or brewing.
History is not made

da chi la pensa e neppure
da chi l'ignora. La storia
non si fa strada, si ostina,
detesta il poco a poco, non procede
né recede, si sposta di binario
e la sua direzione
non è nell'orario.
La storia non giustifica
e non deplora,
la storia non è intrinseca
perché è fuori.
La storia non somministra
carezze o colpi di frusta.
La storia non è magistra
di niente che ci riguardi.
Accorgersene non serve
a farla più vera e più giusta.

II.
La storia non è poi
la devastante ruspa che si dice.
Lascia sottopassaggi, cripte, buche
e nascondigli. C'è chi sopravvive.
La storia è anche benevola: distrugge
quanto più può: se esagerasse, certo
sarebbe meglio, ma la storia è a corto
di notizie, non compie tutte le sue vendette.

La storia gratta il fondo
come una rete a strascico
con qualche strappo e più di un pesce sfugge.
Qualche volta s'incontra l'ectoplasma
d'uno scampato e non sembra particolarmente felice.
Ignora di essere fuori, nessuno glie n'ha parlato.

by those who meditate upon it, nor
by those who ignore it. History
takes no great leaps forward; it is recalcitrant;
it loathes gradualism; it neither progresses
nor regresses. It jumps the track,
and its destinations
are not on any schedule.
History justifies nothing
and laments nothing.
History is in no way intrinsic,
for it is a surrounding.
History does not administer
caresses or whiplashes.
History is not the *magistra*
of any subject having to do with us.
Our knowledge of it will not serve
to make it any truer or more just.

II.
Then again, history isn't
the bulldozer of total devastation people claim.
It leaves underground passages, crypts, holes
and hiding-places. There exist survivors.
History can even be kind: it destroys
as much as it can (and if it went further
so much the better), but history is short
of information and can't always exact revenge.

History drags the bottom
like a net torn here and there
on snags, and more than one fish swims free.
Sometimes you'll meet the living ghost
of an escapee, and he doesn't seem especially happy.
He doesn't know he's outside; nobody told him.

Gli altri, nel sacco, si credono
più liberi di lui.

LE RIME

Le rime sono più noiose delle
dame di San Vincenzo: battono alla porta
e insistono. Respingerle è impossibile
e purché stiano fuori si sopportano.
Il poeta decente le allontana
(le rime), le nasconde, bara, tenta
il contrabbando. Ma le pinzochere ardono
di zelo e prima o poi (rime e vecchiarde)
bussano ancora e sono sempre quelle.

LETTERA

Venezia 19 ..

Il vecchio colonnello di cavalleria
ti offriva negroni bacardi e roederer brut
con l'etichetta rossa. Disse il suo nome ma,
aggiunse, era superfluo ricordarlo.
Non si curò del tuo: del mio meno che meno.
Gli habitués dell'albergo erano tutti amici
anche senza conoscersi: ma soltanto agli sgoccioli
di settembre. Qualcuno ci abbracciava
scambiandoci per altri senza neppure scusarsi,
anzi congratulandosi per il felice errore.
Spuntavano dall'oscuro i grandi, i dimenticati,
la vedova di Respighi, le eredi di Toscanini
un necroforo della Tetrazzini, un omonimo
di Malpighi, Ramerrez- Martinelli,
nube d'argento, e Tullio Carminati,
una gloria per qualche superstite iniziato.

The others, still in the net, believe
themselves more free than he.

THE RHYMES

The rhymes are more annoying
than the charitable Ladies of San Vincenzo: they pound
on the door and insist. Driving them off is impossible,
and as long as they stay outside one puts up with them.
Any decent poet keeps them at a distance
(the rhymes), conceals them, cheats, treats them
as smuggled goods. But those fanatics burn
with zeal, and sooner or later (the rhymes and old bags)
are knocking again, always the same, always cloying.

LETTER

Venice, 19 --

The elderly cavalry colonel
offered you a negroni, a Bacardi, or a glass
of Roederer brut red label. He said his name,
but added there was no need to remember it.
He didn't bother with yours, much less with mine.
The habitués of the hotel, albeit unacquainted,
were all good friends, but only at the tail end
of September. Somebody came to give us a hug,
mistaking us for others, and didn't even apologize,
congratulating himself instead on this happy accident.
The famous and the forgotten leapt out of the shadows:
Respighi's widow, the heirs of Toscanini, an undertaker
who had handled Tetrazzini's funeral, the namesake
of Marcello Malpighi, the tenor Ramerrez/Martinelli
(a cloud of silver hair), the actor Tullio Carminati,
a glorious find for some surviving enthusiast.

(Su tutti il Potestà delle Chiavi, un illustre, persuaso
che noi fossimo i veri e i degni avant le déluge
che poi non venne o fu
poco più di un surplus dell' Acqua Alta).
Il vecchio cavaliere ripeteva da sempre
tra un bourbon e un martini che mai steeplechase
lo vide tra i battuti. E concludeva
sui reumatismi che gli stroncarono le ali.
Si viveva tra eguali, troppo diversi
per detestarsi, ma fin troppo simili
nell'arte del galleggio. L'invitto radoteur
è morto da qualche anno, forse prima di te.
Con lui s'è spento l'ultimo tuo corteggiatore.
Ora all'albergo giungono solo le carovane.
Non più il maestro della liquirizia
al meconio. Più nulla in quello spurgo
di canale. E neppure l' orchestrina
che al mio ingresso dal ponte
mi regalava il pot-pourri dell'ospite
nascosto dietro il paravento: il conte
di Lussemburgo.

LE REVENANT

· ·
quattro sillable, il nome di un ignoto
da te mai più incontrato e senza dubbio morto.
Certamente un pittore; t'ha fatto anche la corte,
lo ammettevi, ma appena: era timido.
Se n'è parlato tra noi molti anni orsono; poi tu
non c'eri piu e ne ho scordato il nome.
Ed ecco una rivista clandestina con volti
e pitture di artisti 'stroncati in boccio'
ai primi del 900. E c'è un suo quadro

(Our illustrious concierge, Keeper of the Keys, believed
we were all the righteous, worthy ones *avant le déluge,*
a flood which never followed, or if it did, was
not much more than an excess of *acqua alta.*)
The old officer kept telling the same stories
between bourbons and martinis, how he never rode
a steeplechase he didn't win, and always ended
by speaking of the rheumatism that clipped his wings.
One lived there among equals, too unalike
to detest one another, but all too similar
in the art of floating along. The undefeated, boring
raconteur died some years ago, perhaps before you did,
and with him the last of your admirers was extinguished.
Now the only ones arriving at the hotel are tour groups.
He's gone, that maestro with his licorice liqueurs
al meconium. There's nothing left to dump in that sewer
of a canal. There's not even the little orchestra
that used to greet me as I stepped off the bridge
into the hotel entrance with a medley requested
by the guest hidden behind a windbreak: *The Count
of Luxembourg.*

LE REVENANT

. . . .
four syllables, the name of some unknown
you never met again, and who is doubtless dead.
Unquestionably a painter; he tried to court you,
you admitted as much, but barely: he was shy.
We spoke of him to each other years ago; then
once you were gone, I forgot the name.
And now here he is, in an underground magazine
among the faces and paintings of artists "nipped
in the bud" in the early 1900s. There's even

orrendo, ma chi puo dirlo? domani sarà un capodopera.
Sei stata forse la sua Clizia senza
saperlo. La notizia non mi rallegra.
Mi chiedo perché i fili di due rocchetti
si sono tanto imbrogliati; e se non sia quel fantasma
l'autentico smarrito e il suo facsimile io.

TEMPO E TEMPI

Non c'è un unico tempo: ci sono molti nastri
che paralleli slittano
spesso in senso contrario e raramente
s'intersecano. È quando si palesa
la sola verità che, disvelata,
viene subito espunta da chi sorveglia
i congegni e gli scambi. E si ripiomba
poi nell'unico tempo. Ma in quell'attimo
solo i pochi viventi si sono riconosciuti
per dirsi addio, non arrivederci.

L'ANGELO NERO

O grande angelo nero
fuligginoso riparami
sotto le tue ali,
che io possa sorradere
i pettini dei pruni, le luminarie dei forni
e inginocchiarmi
sui tizzi spenti se mai
vi resti qualche frangia
delle tue penne

one of his pictures, horrendous, yet who's to say?
Tomorrow maybe they'll call it a masterpiece.
Perhaps you were his Clizia, even if
you never knew. The news doesn't make me happy.
I ask myself how it is that the threads of two spools
can get so entangled; and whether that ghost isn't
the one truly lost and I only his facsimile.

TIME AND TIMES

Time isn't a singular thing: there are many
strands running side by side
often in opposite directions, and they rarely
intersect. It happens when the one sole truth
is made plain, when it reveals itself, only to be
immediately erased by whoever keeps an eye
on the gizmos and gears. And then we fall
back into singular time. But in that moment, the few
souls actually alive recognize each other and say
"farewell." They don't say "until we meet again."

THE BLACK ANGEL

O great black angel
dark as soot, shelter me
beneath your wings
so that I may skim over thorny
brambles, glide above glowing furnaces,
and fall to my knees
upon extinguished embers, assuming
there is anything left
of your tattered plumage

o piccolo angelo buio,
non celestiale né umano,
angelo che traspari
trascolorante difforme
e multiforme, eguale
e ineguale nel rapido lampeggio
della tua incomprensibile fabulazione

o angelo nero disvélati
ma non uccidermi col tuo fulgore,
non dissipare la nebbia che ti aureola,
stàmpati nel mio pensiero
perché non c'è occhio che resista ai fari,
angelo di carbone che ti ripari
dentro lo scialle della caldarrostaia

grande angelo d'ebano
angelo fosco
o bianco, stanco di errare
se ti prendessi un'ala e la sentissi
scricchiolare
non potrei riconoscerti come faccio
nel sonno, nella veglia, nel mattino
perché tra il vero e il falso non una cruna
può trattenere il bipede o il cammello,
e il bruciaticcio, il grumo
che resta sui polpastrelli
è meno dello spolvero
dell'ultima tua piuma, grande angelo
di cenere e di fumo, miniangelo
spazzacamino.

o little dark angel,
neither heavenly nor human,
angel who gleams
with faded colors, deformed
and multiform, the same
and not the same in the rapid flashing
of your incomprehensible fabulation

o black angel unveil yourself
yet do not destroy me with your splendor,
do not dissolve the mist that is your aureole,
but impress yourself upon my thoughts
since there is no eye resistant to your beams,
o coal-black angel, angel who takes cover
under the cloak of a chestnut-vendor's stand

great angel of ebony
angel shadowy
or bright, if I should tire of wandering
and seize you by a wing and hear
its rustling flutter
still I would not know you as I do
in sleep, or wakeful in the night, or at dawn,
since between the true and the false there exists
no needle's eye that might detain biped or camel,
and since the charred residue, the fleck
left sticking to my fingertips
is less substantial than the dust-motes brushed
from your last surviving feather, o great angel
of ashes and smoke, o mini-angel,
chimney sweep.

L'ARNO A ROVEZZANO

I grandi fiumi sono l'immagine del tempo,
crudele e impersonale. Osservati da un ponte
dichiarano la loro nullità inesorabile.
Solo l'ansa esitante di qualche paludoso
giuncheto, qualche specchio
che riluca tra folte sterpaglie e borraccina
può svelare che l'acqua come noi pensa se stessa
prima di farsi vortice e rapina.
Tanto tempo è passato, nulla è scorso
da quando ti cantavo al telefono 'tu
che fai l'addormentata' col triplice cachinno.
La tua casa era un lampo visto dal treno. Curva
sull'Arno come l'albero di Giuda
che voleva proteggerla. Forse c'è ancora o
non è che una rovina. Tutta piena,
mi dicevi, di insetti, inabitabile.
Altro comfort fa per noi ora, altro
sconforto.

LAGGIÙ

La terra sarà sorvegliata
da piattaforme astrali

Più probabili o meno
si faranno laggiù i macelli

Spariranno profeti e profezie
se mai ne furono

Scomparsi l'io il tu il noi il voi
dall'uso

THE ARNO AT ROVEZZANO

Great rivers are the image of time,
cruel and impersonal. Seen from a bridge
they declare their nothingness to be inexorable.
The mere lazy bend beside some swampy
reed-patch, a glassy reflection gleaming
out of scrub growth and moss, can reveal
the way water, like us, thinks about itself
before moving on to whirlpools and destruction.
So much time has gone by and nothing seems past
since I was calling you up to sing that aria, *"tu che fai
l'addormentata,"* complete with its cackles of laughter.
Glimpsed from a train, your house was a flash of light.
It leaned over the river, like the Judas-tree
that attempted to protect it. Maybe it still stands,
or maybe it's nothing but a ruin. Full of flies,
you told me, quite uninhabitable.
It gives us other comfort now, other
discomfort.

DOWN THERE

The earth will be surveilled
from platforms in space

Most likely massacres
will take place down there

Prophets and prophecies will disappear
if they ever existed

Me you us them will fall
out of use

Dire nascita morte inizio fine
sarà tutt'uno

Dire ieri domani
un abuso

Sperare – flatus vocis non compreso
da nessuno

Il Creatore avrà poco da fare
se n'ebbe

I santi poi bisognerà cercarli
tra i cani

. . . .

Gli angeli resteranno inespungibili
refusi.

REBECCA

Ogni giorno di più mi scopro difettivo:
manca il totale.
Gli addendi sono a posto, ineccepibili,
ma la somma?
Rebecca abbeverava i suoi cammelli
e anche se stessa.
Io attendo alla penna e alla gamella
per me e per altri.
Rebecca era assetata, io famelico,
ma non saremo assolti.
Non c'era molt'acqua nell'uadi, forse qualche pozzanghera,
e nella mia cucina poca legna da ardere.

To speak of birth death beginning end
will be all one

To speak of yesterday tomorrow
will be bad grammar

To hope—*flatus vocis* understood
by no one

The Creator will have little to do
if he ever did

As for saints, you'll have to search for them
among the dogs

. . . .

The angels will remain, uncorrectable
misprints

REBECCA

Every day I discover more lacking in myself:
I don't add up to a whole.
The integers are all in place, impeccable,
but the sum total?
Rebecca watered her camels
and provided for herself as well.
I pay attention to my pen and the mess tin
for me and for others.
Rebecca was thirsty, I'm famished,
but neither of us will be found innocent.
There wasn't much water in the *wadi*, maybe a few puddles,
and there's not much firewood for my kitchen stove.

Eppure abbiamo tentato per noi, per tutti, nel fumo,
nel fango con qualche vivente bipede o anche quadrupede.
O mansueta Rebecca che non ho mai incontrata!
Appena una manciata di secoli ci dividono,
un batter d'occhio per chi comprende la tua lezione.
Solo il divino è totale nel sorso e nella briciola,
Solo la morte lo vince se chiede l'intera porzione.

And yet we gave it a try, for ourselves, for everyone, in the
smoke,
in the mud, struggling with a few bipeds or even quadrupeds.
O courteous Rebecca whom I have never met!
A mere handful of centuries separates us, the blink
of an eye for one who comprehends your example.
Only the divine exists complete in a sip, in a crumb.
Only death waits for those who beg for a full portion.

FROM

Diary of '71 and '72 (1973)

(Diario del '71 e '72)

L'ARTE POVERA

La pittura
da cavalletto costa sacrifizi
a chi la fa ed è sempre un sovrappiù
per chi la compra e non sa dove appenderla.
Per qualche anno ho dipinto solo ròccoli
con uccelli insaccati,
su carta blu da zucchero o cannelé da imballo.
Vino e caffè, tracce di dentifricio
se in fondo c'era un mare infiocchettabile,
queste le tinte.
Composi anche con cenere e con fondi
di cappuccino a Sainte-Adresse là dove
Jongkind trovò le sue gelide luci
e il pacco fu protetto da cellofane e canfora
(con scarso esito).
È la parte di me che riesce a sopravvivere
del nulla ch'era in me, del tutto ch'eri
tu, inconsapevole.

I NASCONDIGLI

Quando non sono certo di essere vivo
la certezza è a due passi ma costa pena
ritrovarli gli oggetti, una pipa, il cagnuccio
di legno di mia moglie, un necrologio
del fratello di lei, tre o quattro occhiali
di lei ancora!, un tappo di bottiglia
che colpì la sua fronte in un lontano
cotillon di capodanno a Sils Maria
e altre carabattole. Mutano alloggio, entrano
nei buchi più nascosti, ad ogni ora
hanno rischiato il secchio della spazzatura.
Complottando tra loro si sono organizzati

THE ART POVERA

The painting
on the easel requires sacrifice
from whoever makes it and is never a necessity
for the buyer who must figure out where to hang it.
For a few years all I painted were nets to trap birds,
with a few victims hung in the mesh,
on blue-gray kitchen paper or on wrapping tissue.
Wine and coffee, dabs of toothpaste
if the background was a sea with whitecaps,
these were my pigments.
I painted with ashes, too, and cappuccino
dregs, there in Sainte-Adresse, where
Jongkind found his chilly light,
and I stored the sheaf in cellophane and moth balls
(with poor results).
It's the part of me that managed to survive
of the nothingness I felt inside and the everything
you were and never knew.

HIDING PLACES

Whenever I'm not certain of being alive
reassurance is close at hand, but it takes
effort to find those things again: a pipe, a little
wooden dog that was my wife's, the obituary
of her brother, several pairs of eyeglasses—
hers, too!—a cork that burst from a bottle
long ago and struck her on the forehead
at a ball on New's Years Eve in Sils Maria,
and other knickknacks. They keep moving
around, sneaking into hidey-holes, forever
at risk of being tossed in the scrap basket.
Plotting among themselves, they've arranged

per sostenermi, sanno più di me
il filo che li lega a chi vorrebbe
e non osa disfarsene. Più prossimo
negli anni il Gubelin automatico tenta
di aggregarvisi, sempre rifiutato.
Lo comprammo a Lucerna e lei disse
piove troppo a Lucerna non funzionerà mai.
E infatti...

LA MIA MUSA

La mia Musa è lontana: si direbbe
(è il pensiero dei piú) che mai sia esistita.
Se pure una ne fu, indossa i panni dello spaventacchio
alzato a malapena su una scacchiera di viti.

Sventola come può; ha resistito a monsoni
restando ritta, solo un po' ingobbita.
Se il vento cala sa agitarsi ancora
quasi a dirmi cammina non temere,
finché potrò vederti ti darò vita.

La mia Musa ha lasciato da tempo un ripostiglio
di sartoria teatrale; ed era d'alto bordo
chi di lei si vestiva. Un giorno fu riempita
di me e ne andò fiera. Ora ha ancora una manica
e con quella dirige un suo quartetto
di cannucce. È la sola musica che sopporto.

to sustain me, and they know more than I
about the ties that bind them to a man
who'd like to be rid of them but doesn't dare.
In recent years, my self-winding Gübelin
watch has tried to join the conspirators, but
is always rebuffed. We bought it in Lucerne,
and she told me: "It rains too much
in Lucerne, it will never work right."
And in fact ...

MY MUSE

My muse is so far away now you might say
(it's what most people think) she never existed.
If she ever did, she's been dressed as a scarecrow
and raised barely above a grid of grapevines.

She flaps in the wind as best she can, standing
up under monsoons, just a tad hunched over.
When the wind dies, she still knows how to stir,
as if to tell me: "Don't be afraid to go on, so long
as you're within my sight I will give you life."

My muse left a theater wardrobe quite some
time ago, and those dressed in her costume
used to be high class. There was a day that role
was filled by me, and with me she went in style.
Now she has one sleeve left and uses it to conduct
a panpipe quartet. It's the only music I can bear.

IL FUOCO

Siamo alla Pentecoste e non c'è modo
che scendano dal cielo lingue di fuoco.
Eppure un Geremia apparso sul video
aveva detto che ormai sarà questione di poco.
Di fuoco non si vede nulla, solo
qualche bombetta fumogena all'angolo di via Bigli.
Questi farneticanti in doppiopetto o in sottana
non sembrano molto informati del loro mortifero aspetto.
Il fuoco non viene dall'alto ma dal basso,
non s'è mai spento, non è mai cresciuto,
nessuno l'ha mai veduto, fuochista o vulcanologo.
Chi se ne accorge non dà l'allarme, resta muto.
Gli uccelli di malaugurio non sono più creduti.

A QUESTO PUNTO

A questo punto smetti
dice l'ombra.
T'ho accompagnato in guerra e in pace e anche
nell'intermedio,
sono stata per te l'esaltazione e il tedio,
t'ho insufflato virtù che non possiedi,
vizi che non avevi. Se ora mi stacco
da te non avrai pena, sarai lieve
più delle foglie, mobile come il vento.
Devo alzare la maschera, io sono il tuo pensiero,
sono il tuo in-necessario, l'inutile tua scorza.
A questo punto smetti, stràppati dal mio fiato
e cammina nel cielo come un razzo.
C'è ancora qualche lume all'orizzonte
e chi lo vede non è un pazzo, è solo
un uomo e tu intendevi di non esserlo
per amore di un'ombra. T'ho ingannato

FIRE

We've come to Pentecost, and there's no way
tongues of fire can descend from the sky.
And yet a Jeremiah appeared on the screen
to prophesy that it won't be long now.
As for fire, there's none visible, just a few
smoke bombs down at the corner of Via Bigli.
These ravers in double-breasted suits and cassocks
seem poorly informed as to their lethal expectations.
The fire won't come from on high, but from
below—it's never gone out, never flared up,
no one's seen it, no furnace stoker or volcanologist.
Those aware of it raise no alarms, they keep quiet.
Birds of ill omen aren't believed nowadays.

AT THIS POINT

At this point stop
says the shadow.
I kept you company in war and peace and also
in the intervals between,
I was your exaltation and your tedium,
I puffed you full of virtue you never possessed,
and vices you never had. If I leave you now
it won't pain you, you'll feel lighter
than the leaves, as free as the wind.
It's time to remove my mask: I'm your own thought,
I'm a non-necessity, your useless outer shell.
At this point stop, tear yourself free of my breath
and stride across the sky like a missile in flight.
There's still a bit of glow on the horizon,
and the person who sees it isn't insane, he's
merely a man, which you tried not to be
for love of a shadow. I deceived you,

ma ora ti dico a questo punto smetti.
Il tuo peggio e il tuo meglio non t'appartengono
e per quello che avrai puoi fare a meno
di un'ombra. A questo punto
guarda con i tuoi occhi e anche senz'occhi.

LA PENDOLA A CARILLON

La vecchia pendola a carillon
veniva dalla Francia forse dal tempo
del secondo Impero.
Non dava trilli o rintocchi ma esalava
più che suonare tanto n'era fioca la voce
l'entrata di Escamillo o le campane
di Corneville: le novità di quando
qualcuno l'acquistò: forse il proavo
finito al manicomio e sotterrato
senza rimpianti, necrologi o altre
notizie che turbassero i suoi non nati nepoti.
I quali vennero poi e vissero senza memoria
di chi portò quell'oggetto tra inospiti mura sferzate
da furibonde libecciate – e chi
di essi ne udì il richiamo ? Era una sveglia
beninteso che mai destò nessuno
che non fosse già sveglio. Io solo un'alba
regolarmente insonne traudii l'ectoplasma
vocale, il soffio della toriada,
ma appena per un attimo. Poi la voce
della boîte non si estinse ma si fece parola
poco udibile e disse non c'è molla né carica
che un giorno non si scarichi. Io ch'ero
il Tempo lo abbandono. Ed a te che sei l'unico
mio ascoltatore dico cerca di vivere
nel fuordeltempo, quello che nessuno

but at this point I'm telling you to stop.
Neither your worst nor your best belong to you,
and to get what's coming, you can do without
a shadow. At this point
look with your own eyes—and look without eyes, too.

THE CLOCK WITH THE CARILLON CHIMES

The old pendulum clock with the carillon chimes
came from France, possibly at the time
of the Second Empire.
So faint was its voice it didn't ring or toll,
and it exhaled rather than played
Escamillo's entrance aria or *Les cloches
de Corneville*, novelties of the era when
it was purchased, possibly by that ancestor
who wound up in the madhouse and was buried
without regrets or obituaries or other announcement
which might disturb his as yet unborn descendants.
Those came after and lived without any memory
of whoever brought it into their inhospitable home
lashed by the fierce *libeccio* wind—and who
among them ever heard it ring? Its alarm,
of course, could never rouse anyone
not already awake. I alone, once in the dawn,
insomniac as usual, detected its ghostly
melody, its breath of the bullfighter's song,
but only for an instant. And then the voice
in the clock-case didn't die but sank to a whisper
and said: "No mechanism or tension exists
that won't run down someday, and I who was
Time itself hereby abandon time. To you,
the only one listening, I say try to live
in timelessness, the thing which no one

può misurare.» Poi la voce tacque
e l'orologio per molti anni ancora
rimase appeso al muro. Probabilmente
v'è ancora la sua traccia sull'intonaco.

I NUOVI ICONOGRAFI

Si sta allestendo l'iconografia
dei massimi scrittori e presto anche
dei minimi. Vedremo dove hanno abitato,
se in regge o in bidonvilles, le loro scuole
e latrine se interne o appiccicate
all'esterno con tubi penzolanti
su stabbi di maiali, studieremo gli oroscopi
di ascendenti, propaggini e discendenti,
le strade frequentate, i lupanari se mai
ne sopravviva alcuno all'onorata Merlin,
toccheremo i loro abiti, gli accappatoi, i clisteri
se usati e quando e quanti, i menù degli alberghi,
i pagherò firmati, le lozioni
o pozioni o decotti, la durata
dei loro amori, eterei o carnivori
o solo epistolari, leggeremo
cartelle cliniche, analisi e se cercassero il sonno
nel Baffo o nella Biblia.
                              Così la storia
trascura gli epistemi per le emorroidi
mentre vessilli olimpici sventolano sui pennoni
e sventole di mitraglia forniscono i contorni.

can measure." Whereupon its voice ceased
entirely, though for many more years
the clock still hung on the wall. Probably
there's still some shadow of it on the plaster.

THE NEW ICONOGRAPHERS

It's underway, the exposition of the icons
of the great writers, and before long even
the minor ones. We'll be shown where they lived,
if in palaces or in slums, see their schools,
their toilets, whether in-house or in shacks
outside with pipes running down
to the pigpen; we'll study the horoscopes
of their ancestors, offspring, and descendants,
the streets they frequented, the bordellos
(if any have managed to survive the legislation
of the honorary senator Merlin); we'll touch
their clothes, their bathrobes, know if they
used enemas (and if so how many and when);
we'll finger the menus of their hotel dining rooms,
the IOUs they signed, their lotions, potions,
their decoctions; we'll determine the length
of their love affairs, be they ethereal or flesh-devouring
or purely epistolary; we'll read their medical charts
and test results and know if they sought sleep
in Baffo or in the Bible.
                    Thus will literary history
overlook learning in favor of hemorrhoids,
while Olympic flags are flying and bursts
of machine gun fire provide the atmosphere.

Non ho amato mai molto la montagna
e detesto le Alpi. Le Ande, le Cordigliere
non le ho vedute mai. Pure la Sierra
de Guadarrama mi ha rapito, dolce
com'è l'ascesa e in vetta daini, cervi
secondo le notizie dei dépliants turistici.
Solo l'elettrica aria dell'Engadina
ci vinse, mio insettino, ma non si era
tanto ricchi da dirci hic manebimus.
Tra i laghi solo quello di Sorapis
fu la grande scoperta. C'era la solitudine
delle marmotte più udite che intraviste
e l'aria dei Celesti; ma quale strada
per accedervi? Dapprima la percorsi
da solo per vedere se i tuoi occhietti
potevano addentrarsi tra cunicoli
zigzaganti tra lastre alte di ghiaccio.
E così lunga! Confortata solo
nel primo tratto, in folti di conifere,
dallo squillo d'allarme delle ghiandaie.
Poi ti guidai tenendoti per mano
fino alla cima, una capanna vuota.
Fu quello il nostro lago, poche spanne d'acqua,
due vite troppo giovani per essere vecchie,
e troppo vecchie per sentirsi giovani.
Scoprimmo allora che cos'è l'età.
Non ha nulla a che fare col tempo, è qualcosa che dice
che ci fa dire siamo qui, è un miracolo
che non si può ripetere. Al confronto
la gioventù è il più vile degl'inganni.

I've never loved the mountains much,
and I loathe the Alps. The Andes, the Rockies,
I never went to see them. True, the Guadarrama
Sierras swept me away, with their gentle slopes,
the wildlife at their peaks, fallow deer and elk
according to the notes in the tourist brochures.
And the electric atmosphere of the Engadin Valley
was the one air that enraptured us, my little Mosca,
but we weren't so well off as to say *hic manebimus*.
As for mountain lakes, Sorapis, in the Dolomites,
was our great discovery. There we found solitude
among the marmots, heard more than glimpsed,
and blue skies fit for Celestial Beings. But what
path could lead us up? At first I walked it
by myself, to check if your weak eyes
could cope with the switchback road
that burrowed through the ice-bound cliffs.
And such a long way! A road comfortable only
in the first stretch, among dense conifers
and the alarm cries of the perturbed jays.
After that, I led you by the hand
all the way to the top and an empty hut.
There was our lake, just a few feet of water,
where we were two lives too young to be old
but too old to feel we were young.
That's when we learned what aging is.
Nothing to do with time, it's something that tells us,
that makes us tell ourselves: "Here we are,
it's a miracle and won't come again." By comparison
youth is the most contemptible of illusions.

Four-Year Notebook (1978)

(Quaderno di Quattro Anni)

L'ONORE

a Guido Piovene

Un giorno mi dicevi
che avresti ritenuto grande onore
lucidare le scarpe
di Cecco Beppe il vecchio Imperatore.
Si era presso il confine ma non oltre
la terra delle chiacchere in cui sei nato.
Mi dichiarai d'accordo anche se un giorno
senza sparare un colpo
della mia Webley Scott 7,65
senza uccidere senza possedere
neanche un'ombra dell'arte militare
avevo fatto fronte ai pochi stracci
dell'oste avversa. Ma mi chiesi pure
quale fosse la briciola d'onore
che mi era scivolata tra le dita
e non me n'ero accorto. C'è sempre un paio di stivali
che attendono la spazzola il lustrino,
c'è sempre il punto anche se impercettibile
per il quale si può senza sprecarla
usare una parola come onore.
Non è questione di stivali o altri
imbiancamenti di sepolcri. Il fatto è
che l'onore ci appare quando è impossibile,
quando somiglia come due gocce d'acqua
al suo gemello, la vergogna. Un lampo
tra due confini non territoriali,
una luce che abbuia tutto il resto
questo è l'onore che non abbiamo avuto
perché la luce non è fatta solo
per gli occhi. È questo il mio ricordo, il solo
che nasce su un confine e non lo supera.

HONOR

for Guido Piovene

One day you told me
you would have held it a great honor
just to shine the shoes
of Cecco Beppe, the old emperor.
We were a few feet this side of the frontier
in that gossipy region where you were born.
I declared I agreed, even if there'd been a day
when, without firing a shot
from my Webley Scott 7.65,
without killing anyone or possessing
the slightest hint of military ability,
I confronted a few ragged soldiers
of the opposing army. But I asked myself
what the scrap of honor might be, really,
that had slipped between my fingers
while I was unaware. There's always a pair of boots
waiting for the polish and brush;
there's always a moment, even if imperceptible,
concerning which one may pronounce
a word like honor without debasement.
But it's not a matter of boots or fresh coats
of whitewash on sepulchers. The fact is
honor appears to us when it's impossible,
when it's as like as two drops of water
to its twin, disgrace. A flash of light
where two unearthly frontiers meet,
an illumination that puts all else in the shade:
that's what honor is, and it isn't ours,
because its illumination isn't created
for the eyes alone. And that's my memory, the lone
one born on a border it never will cross.

LA SOLITUDINE

Se mi allontano due giorni
i piccioni che beccano
sul davanzale
entrano in agitazione
secondo i loro obblighi corporativi.
Al mio ritorno l'ordine si rifà
con supplemento di briciole
e disappunto del merlo che fa la spola
tra il venerato dirimpettaio e me.
A così poco è ridotta la mia famiglia.
E c'è chi n'ha una o due, che spreco ahimè!

L'EROISMO

Clizia mi suggeriva di ingaggiarmi
tra i guerriglieri di Spagna e più di una volta mi sento
morto a Guadalajara o superstite illustre
che mal reggesi in piede dopo anni di galera.
Ma nulla di ciò avvenne: nemmeno il torrentizio
verbo del comiziante redimito di gloria
e d'altri incarchi mi regalò la sorte.
Ma dove ho combattuto io che non amo
il gregge degli inani e dei fuggiaschi?
Qualche cosa ricordo. Un prigioniero *mio*
che aveva in tasca un Rilke e fummo amici
per pochi istanti; e inutili fatiche
e tonfi di bombarde e il fastidioso
ticchettìo dei cecchini.
Ben poco e anche inutile per lei
che non amava le patrie e n'ebbe una per caso.

SOLITUDE

If I go away for a couple of days
the pigeons that feed
on my windowsill
become agitated
as to their bodily requirements.
Upon my return order is restored
with some additional breadcrumbs
and the frustration of the blackbird
who shuttles between me and the old man
in the building across from mine.
That's how small now my little family is.
Some have one or two and, ah me, what a waste.

HEROISM

Clizia suggested I enroll myself
among the partisans in Spain, and more than once I felt
I'd died at Guadalajara or was an honored survivor
unsteady on my feet after my years in prison.
But nothing like that occurred: fate did not even
give me the river of words of a rabble-rousing orator
whose speech is crowned with glory and high office.
Then where did I fight, who have never loved
the inane herd of the foolish and the fugitive?
I recall a couple of things. A prisoner of *mine*
with Rilke in his pocket, making us friends
for a few moments; and the useless busywork
and the thud of the bombs and the annoying
rat-a-tat of the snipers.
Nothing much, and useless to her, who felt no love
for Fatherlands and had one only by chance.

LEGGENDO KAVAFIS

Mentre Nerone dorme placido nella sua
traboccante bellezza
i suoi piccoli lari che hanno udito
le voci delle Erinni lasciano il focolare
in grande confusione. Come e quando
si desterà? Così disse il Poeta.
Io, sovrano di nulla, neppure di me stesso,
senza il tepore di odorosi legni
e lambito dal gelo di un aggeggio
a gasolio,
io pure ascolto suoni tictaccanti
di zoccoli e di piedi, ma microscopici.
Non mi sveglio, ero desto già da un pezzo
e non mi attendo ulteriori orrori
oltre i già conosciuti.
Neppure posso imporre a qualche famulo
di tagliarsi le vene. Nulla mi turba. Ho udito
lo zampettìo di un topolino. Trappole
non ne ho mai possedute.

PER UN FIORE RECISO

Spenta in tenera età
può dirsi che hai reso diverso il mondo?
Questa è per me certezza che non posso
comunicare ad altri. Non si è mai certi
di noi stessi che pure abbiamo occhi
e mani per vederci, per toccarci.
Una traccia invisibile non è per questo
meno segnata? Te lo dissi un giorno
e tu: è un fatto che non mi riguarda.
Sono la capinera che dà un trillo

READING CAVAFY

While Nero sleeps placidly amid his
over-the-top gorgeous decor
his little household gods have heard
the sound of the approaching Furies and flee
his hearth in great confusion. How and when
will the emperor awake? So writes the Poet.
I, sovereign of nothing, not even of myself,
lacking the warmth of a fragrant fire
and lit by the chill glow of a contraption
that burns fuel oil,
I, too, hear tippy-taps that sound
like hooves and feet, but they're minuscule.
I don't wake up, I've been awake for hours,
and I don't foresee any horrors beyond
the ones I already know.
I haven't the power to force some servant
to cut his veins. I'm unalarmed. What I heard
was the scamper of a mouse. Traps
are things I've never owned.

FOR A CUT FLOWER

Dead at a tender age,
could one say you changed the world?
For me, that's a certainty I can't
communicate to others. We're never sure
of our own existence, though we have eyes
to see ourselves and hands with which to touch.
And doesn't this make an unseen imprint
even harder to detect? So I told you
one day, and your response: it's a fact
that has nothing to do with me.
I'm the blackcap that trills its song

e a volte lo ripete ma non si sa
se è quella o un'altra. E non potresti farlo
neanche te che hai orecchio.

IL FUOCO E IL BUIO

Qualche volta la polvere da sparo
non prende fuoco per umidità,
altre volte s'accende senza il fiammifero
o l'acciarino.
Basterebbe il tascabile briquet
se ci fosse una goccia di benzina.
E infine non occorre fuoco affatto,
anzi un buon sottozero tiene a freno
la tediosa bisava, l'Ispirazione.
Non era troppo arzilla giorni fa
ma incerottava bene le sue rughe.
Ora pare nascosta tra le pieghe
della tenda e ha vergogna di se stessa.
Troppe volte ha mentito, ora può scendere
sulla pagina il buio il vuoto il niente.
Di questo puoi fidarti amico scriba.
Puoi credere nel buio quando la luce mente.

SOLILOQUIO

Il canale scorre silenzioso
maleodorante
questo è il palazzo dove fu composto
il Tristano
ed ecco il buco dove Henry James
gustò le crêpes suzette –
non esitono più i grandi uomini

and sometimes trills again, but no one knows
if it's the same bird or another. And you couldn't
tell, either, even if you do have an ear.

FIRE AND DARKNESS

Sometimes the gunpowder
is damp and won't catch fire,
other times it explodes without a match
or spark from a flint.
A pocket lighter would be enough
if you had a few drops of butane.
In the end, you don't need fire at all,
quite the opposite, a nice sub-zero
cold-snap puts the brakes on that tedious
great-grandmother, Inspiration.
She wasn't any too spry the other day,
but she managed to paint over her wrinkles.
Now, though, she seems to be hiding
behind the curtains, ashamed of herself.
She's lied too many times, and now it can fall
on the page: darkness, nothingness, the void.
Have faith in that, my Scribbling Friend.
You can trust the dark when light deceives.

SOLILOQUY

The canal flows by silently
malodorously
this is the palace that saw the composition
of *Tristan and Isolde*
and there's the hole-in-the-wall where Henry James
enjoyed his *crêpes suzette*—
Great Men don't exist any longer

ne restano inattendibili biografie
nessuno certo scriverà la mia –
gli uomini di San Giorgio sono più importanti
di tanti altri e di me ma non basta non basta –
il futuro ha appetito non si contenta più
di hors-d'œuvre e domanda schidionate
di volatili frolli, nauseabonde delizie –
il futuro è altresì disappetente
può volere una crosta ma che crosta
quale non fu mai vista nei menus –
il futuro è anche onnivoro e non guarda
per il sottile – Qui è la casa dove
visse più anni un pederasta illustre
assassinato altrove –Il future è per lui –
non è nulla di simile nella mia vita
nulla che sazi le bramose fauci
del futuro.

"LA CAPINERA NON FU UCCISA"

La capinera non fu uccisa
da un cacciatore ch'io sappia.
Morì forse nel mezzo del mattino. E non n'ebbi
mai notizia. Suppongo che di me
abbia perduto anche il ricordo. Se ora
qualche fantasma aleggia qui d'attorno
non posso catturarlo per chiedergli chi sei?
Può darsi che i fantasmi non abbiano più consistenza
di un breve soffio di vento. Uno di questi rèfoli
potrei essere anch'io senza saperlo: labile
al punto che la messa in scena di cartone
che mi circonda può restare in piedi.
Ben altri soffi occorrono per distruggerla.

all that's left are unreliable biographies
and certainly no one will write my own—
the scholars you'll find on San Giorgio
are more distinguished than me or many others
but it's not enough, it's not enough—
the future is hungry now and won't be satisfied
with *hors-d'œuvres*, it wants breaded gamebirds
en brochette, delicacies to make the gorge rise—
and yet sometimes the future has no appetite at all
it can ask for just a crust ... but what a crust!
a thing never seen on menus anywhere—
actually the future is omnivorous and it isn't
dainty—Look, here's the house in which
an illustrious pederast murdered elsewhere
lived for many years—the future belongs to him—
I've nothing like that to offer in my own life
nothing that might satisfy the rapacious jaws
of the future.

"THE BLACKCAP WASN'T KILLED"

The blackcap wasn't killed
by a hunter, so far as I know.
Perhaps she died mid-morning. And I never
got the news. Regarding me, I suppose
she had lost all recollection. If some
ghostly presence flutters around here now,
I can't capture it to ask: "Who are you?"
It may be that ghosts have no more substance
than a faint breath of wind. Perhaps I, too,
am just one of these puffs and don't know it,
a breeze so light the cardboard stage-set
that surrounds me manages to stand upright.
To destroy it will take different gusts entirely.

Dove potranno allora rifugiarsi
questi errabondi veli? Non c'è scienza
filosofia teologia che se ne occupi.

DOMANDE SENZA RISPOSTA

Mi chiedono se ho scritto
un canzoniere d'amore
e se il mio onlie begetter
è uno solo o è molteplice.
Ahimè,
la mia testa è confusa, molte figure
vi si addizionano,
ne formano una sola che discerno
a malapena nel mio crepuscolo.
Se avessi posseduto
un liuto come d'obbligo
per un trobar meno chiuso
non sarebbe difficile
dare un nome a colei che ha posseduto
la mia testa poetica o altro ancora.
Se il nome
fosse una conseguenza delle cose,
di queste non potrei dirne una sola
perché le cose sono fatti e i fatti
in prospettiva sono appena cenere.
Non ho avuto purtroppo che la parola,
qualche cosa che approssima ma non tocca;
e così
non c'è depositaria del mio cuore
che non sia nella bara. Se il suo nome
fosse un nome o più nomi non conta nulla
per chi è rimasto fuori, ma per poco,

Where will they take refuge then, these stray
bits of gossamer? There exists no science,
philosophy, theology that concerns itself with them.

QUESTIONS WITHOUT AN ANSWER

They ask me if I have written
a cycle of Petrarchan love poems
and if my "onlie begetter"
is one muse or many.
Ah me,
my mind's a confusion, and many figures
pile up there
to form the single shape that I
can barely make out in my twilight.
If I had ever possessed
a lute like the ones that are standard issue
for troubadours less given to *trobar clus*,
it wouldn't be difficult
to give a name to the woman who possessed
my poetic thoughts and much else besides.
If the name
was the consequence of things,
still I couldn't choose just one among them,
because things are facts and facts
seen in perspective are only ashes.
All I've ever had, alas, is language,
a thing that approximates but can't truly touch,
and thus
there exists no keeper of my heart
who is not in the grave. Whether her name
is one or many means nothing
to a person left outside—though not for long—

della divina inesistenza. A presto,
adorate mie larve!

Le Muse stanno appollaiate
sulla balaustrata
appena un filo di brezza sull'acqua
c'è qualche albero illustre
la magnolia il cipresso l'ippocastano
la vecchia villa è scortecciata
da un vetro rotto vedo sofà ammuffiti
e un tavolo da ping-pong. Qui non viene nessuno
da molti anni. Un guardiano era previsto
ma si sa come vanno le previsioni.
È strana l'angoscia che si prova
in questa deserta proda sabbiosa erbosa
dove i salici piangono davvero
e ristagna indeciso tra vita e morte
un intermezzo senza pubblico. È
un'angoscia limbale sempre incerta
tra la catastrofe e l'apoteosi
di una rigogliosa decrepitudine.
Se il bandolo del puzzle più tormentoso
fosse più che un'ubbia
sarebbe strano trovarlo dove neppure un'anguilla
tenta di sopravvivere. Molti anni fa c'era qui
una famiglia inglese. Purtroppo manca il custode
ma forse quegli angeli (angli) non erano così pazzi
da essere custoditi.

the divine non-existence. See you soon,
my beloved ghosts!

BESIDE LAKE ORTA

The Muses stand perched
on the balustrade
a breath of wind barely ripples the water
there are a few specimen trees
a magnolia a cypress a horse-chestnut
the old villa's paint is peeling
through a broken pane I see moldy sofas
and a ping-pong table. Not a soul has come here
for many years. A watchman was to be provided
but you know how such provisions turn out.
Strange, the anguish one feels
on this weedy, sandy, deserted shore
where the willows weep for real
and a listless intermezzo without an audience
hovers undecided between life and death. It is
a stagnant anguish, a liminal state
of lush decrepitude forever poised
between catastrophe and apotheosis.
If the key to the riddle that torments us most
lies in anything other than a scary story,
how strange to find it in a place where not even an eel
would try to survive. Many years ago there was
an English family living here. Without a guardian, sadly,
but maybe those angels (Anglos) weren't so daft
that a guardian was required.

IN UNA CITTÀ DEL NORD

Come copia dell'Eden primigenio
manca il confronto con l'originale.
Certo vale qualcosa. Gli scoiattoli
saltano su trapezi di rami alti.
Rari i bambini, ognuno di più padri o madri.
Anche se non fa freddo c'è aria di ghiacciaia.
A primavera si dovrà difendersi
dalle volpi o da altre bestie da pelliccia.
Così mi riferisce il mio autista
navarrese o gallego portato qui dal caso.
Non gli va giù la democrácia. Tale
e quale il Marqués de Villanova.
Io guardo e penso o fingo. Si paga a caro prezzo
un'anima moderna. Potrei anche provarmici.

DI UN GATTO SPERDUTO

Il povero orfanello
non s'era ancora inselvatichito
se fu scacciato dal condominio
perché non lacerasse le moquettes con gli unghielli.
Me ne ricordo ancora passando per quella via
dove accaddero fatti degni di storia
ma indegni di memoria. Fors'è che qualche briciola
voli per conto suo.

IPOTESI

Nella valle di Armageddon
Iddio e il diavolo conversano
pacificamente dei loro affari.
Nessuno dei due ha interesse
a uno scontro decisivo.

IN A NORTHERN CITY

As a copy of our progenitors' Garden of Eden,
well, we lack the original for comparison,
but it's certainly acceptable. Squirrels leap
from their trapezes, branches high overhead.
A very few children, each with more than one parent.
Even if it isn't cold out, the air feels glacial.
In springtime, one has to guard oneself
against foxes and other furry creatures.
That's what my driver tells me, brought here
by chance from Galicia or Navarre.
He can't stomach *democrácia*. Which is just
how the Marqués de Villanova would put it.
I stare off and pretend I'm thinking. You pay a high price
for the modern soul. I might even give it a try.

ABOUT A LOST CAT

The poor little orphan
hadn't yet gone feral
but was chased from the apartment block
so his tiny claws wouldn't shred the carpets.
I still recall him, walking down that street
where incidents occurred worthy of history
but unworthy of memory. Maybe some scraps
of recollection take wing on their own.

HYPOTHESIS

In the Valley of Armageddon
the Lord and the devil discuss
their affairs peacefully.
Neither of the two has any interest
in a decisive battle.

L'Apocalissi sarebbe
da prendersi con le molle?
È più che certo ma questo
non può insegnarsi nelle scuole.
Io stesso fino da quando
ero alunno delle elementari
credevo di essere un combattente
dalla parte giusta.
Gli insegnanti erano miti, non frustavano.
Gli scontri erano posti nell'ovatta,
incruenti, piacevoli. Il peggio
era veduto in prospettiva. Quello
che più importava era che il soccombente
fosse dall'altra parte.
Così passarono gli anni, troppi e inutili.
Fu sparso molto sangue che non fecondò i campi.
Eppure la parte giusta era lì, a due palmi
e non fu mai veduta. Fosse mai accaduto
il miracolo nulla era più impossibile
dell'esistenza stessa di noi uomini.
Per questo nella valle di Armageddon
non accadono mai risse e tumulti.

SENZA PERICOLO

Il filosofo interdisciplinare
è quel tale che ama *se vautrer*
(vuol dire stravaccarsi) nel più fetido
lerciume consumistico. E il peggio è
che lo fa con suprema voluttà
e ovviamente dall'alto di una cattedra
già da lui disprezzata.
                    Non s'era visto mai
che un naufrago incapace di nuotare

Is the Apocalypse something
to be handled with tongs?
That's more than certain, but
it's not what's taught in class.
I myself, ever since I was a pupil
in elementary school,
believed I was a combatant
fighting on the side of the just.
The teachers were gentle, they didn't hit us.
The battles came buffered in padding,
bloodless, even pleasant. Awful things
were put in perspective. What mattered
was that the losers in the show-down
should be on the other side.
And so years passed, too many and unavailing.
A lot of blood was spilled that fertilized no fields.
And yet the side of the just did exist, close at hand,
even if never seen. Had the miracle ever occurred,
nothing would have been more impossible
than the sheer existence of us human beings.
That's why in the Valley of Armageddon
there aren't any brawls or melees.

IN NO DANGER

The interdisciplinary scholar
is the sort that loves *se vautrer*
(i.e. to wallow) in the most disgusting
market-oriented filth. The worst of it is
he does so with voluptuous delight
and of course, from the height of a university
chair he has long since come to despise.
                          No one ever saw
a shipwrecked sailor who's unable to swim

delirasse di gioia mentre la nave
colava a picco. Ma non c'è pericolo
per gli uomini pneumatici e lui lo sa.

ASPASIA

A tarda notte gli uomini
entravano nella sua stanza
dalla finestra. Si era a pianterreno.
L'avevo chiamata Aspasia e n'era contenta.
Poi ci lasciò. Fu barista, parrucchiera e altro.
Raramente accadeva d'incontrarla.
Chiamavo allora Aspasia! a gran voce
e lei senza fermarsi sorrideva.
Eravamo coetanei, sarà morta da un pezzo.
Quando entrerò nell'inferno, quasi per abitudine
griderò Aspasia alla prima ombra che sorrida.
Lei tirerà di lungo naturalmente. Mai
sapremo chi fu e chi non fu
quella farfalla che aveva appena un nome
scelto da me.

"PROTEGGETEMI"

Proteggetemi
custodi miei silenziosi
perché il sole si raffredda
e l'ultima foglia dell'alloro
era polverosa
e non servì nemmeno per la casseruola
dell'arrosto -
proteggetemi da questa pellicola
da quattro soldi
che continua a svolgersi

delirious with joy to watch his boat go down.
But hot air floats, and there's no danger
for human gasbags, and our professor knows it.

ASPASIA

Late at night the men
used to enter her room
through the window. It was on the ground floor.
I used to call her Aspasia and it made her happy.
Then she left us. She worked as a barmaid,
a hairdresser, other things. Occasionally
I happened to run into her.
"Aspasia!" I'd cry out to her then in a loud voice,
and she'd smile without stopping.
We were coevals, she probably died a while ago.
When I enter into hell, almost out of habit,
I'll scream "Aspasia" at the first smiling shade I see.
She'll sidle off quickly of course. We'll never
know who she was and who she wasn't,
that butterfly who possessed no more than a name
I chose for her myself.

"PROTECT ME"

Protect me
o you my silent guardians
because the sun grows cold
and the last laurel leaf
was covered in dust
and no good even for cooking leftovers—
protect me from this two-bit movie
that continues to play

davanti a me
e pretende di coinvolgermi
come attore o comparsa
non prevista dal copione -
proteggetemi persino
dalla vostra presenza
quasi sempre inutile
e intempestiva
proteggetemi
dalle vostre spaventose assenze -
dal vuoto che create
attorno a me
proteggetemi dalle Muse
che vidi appollaiate
o anche dimezzate a mezzo busto
per nascondersi meglio
dal mio passo di fantasma -
proteggetemi o meglio ancora
ignoratemi
quando entrerò nel loculo
che ho già pagato da anni -
proteggetemi dalla fama/farsa
che mi ha introdotto nel Larousse illustrato
per scancellarmi poi
dalla nuova edizione -
proteggetemi
da chi impetra la vostra permanenza
attorno al mio catafalco -
proteggetemi con la vostra dimenticanza
se questo può servire a tenermi in piedi
poveri lari sempre chiusi nella vostra
dubbiosa identità -
proteggetemi senza che alcuno
ne sia informato

before my eyes
and claims I am in it
as an actor or extra
uncalled for by the script—
protect me even
from your presence
almost always useless
and ill-timed
protect me from your terrifying absences—
from the emptiness you create
around me
protect me from the Muses
I saw lined up like roosting birds
or even shrunk to shoulder busts
the better to conceal themselves
from my ghostly passage—
protect me or better yet
ignore me
the day I enter the burial niche
I purchased years ago—
protect me from the fame and/or farce
that got me into the illustrated Larousse
only to see me deleted
from the subsequent edition—
protect me from anyone who pleads
for your eternal attention to my catafalque—
protect me with your forgetting
if it serves to keep me on my feet
o you poor *lares* forever imprisoned
in your dubious identity—
protect me without anyone
hearing of it

perché il sole si raffredda e chi lo sa
malvagiamente se ne rallegra
o miei piccoli numi
divinità di terz'ordine scacciate
dall'etere.

LUNGOLAGO

Campione

Il piccolo falco pescatore
sfrecciò e finì in un vaso di terracotta
fra i tanti di un muretto del lungolago.
Nascosto nei garofani era visibile
quel poco da non rendere impossibile
un dialogo.
Sei l'ultimo esemplare di una specie
che io credevo estinta, così dissi.
Ma la sovrabbondanza di vuoi uomini
sortirà eguale effetto mi fu risposto.
Ora apprendo osservai che si è troppi o nessuno.
Col privilegio vostro disse il falchetto
che qualcuno di voi vedrà il balletto finale.
A meno ribattei che tempo e spazio, fine
e principio non siano invenzioni umane
mentre tu col tuo becco hai divorato il Tutto.
Addio uomo, addio falco dimentica la tua pesca.
E tu scorda la tua senza becco e senz'ali,
omiciattolo, ometto.
                    E il furfante dispare in un alone
de porpora e di ruggine.

because the sun grows cold and those who know
respond with malevolent joy
o my little divinities
third-rate godlets driven out
of the ethereal.

LAKESIDE DRIVE

Campione

The small fish hawk
sailed off to perch on a terracotta vase,
one of many on the low wall by the lakeside drive.
Hidden among the carnations, he was just
visible enough so that dialogue
wasn't impossible.
You're the last survivor of a species
I thought extinct, is what I said.
Yes, but the overpopulation of you men
dooms you to the same fate, was the reply.
Now I grasp, I observed, that we must exist
as either too many or none at all.
With the difference, said the hawk, that one among you
will be privileged to witness the last dance.
Assuming, I shot back, that time and space, beginning
and end, aren't merely human inventions, whereas
you with your beak have fed on the Whole of Existence.
Farewell man. Farewell hawk, forget about your fishing.
And you forget your fishing minus wings and beak,
O little man, homunculus.
                    And the rascal disappeared
into a halo of russet and maroon.

Non sempre o quasi mai la nostra identità personale coincide
col tempo misurabile dagli strumenti che abbiamo.
La sala è grande, ha fregi e stucchi barocchi
e la vetrata di fondo rivela un biondo parco di Stiria,
con qualche nebbiolina che il sole dissolve.
L'interno è puro Vermeer più piccolo e più vero
del vero ma di uno smalto incorruttibile.
A sinistra una bimba vestita da paggio
tutta trine e ricami fino al ginocchio
sta giocando col suo adorato scimmiotto.
A destra la sorella di lei maggiore, Arabella,
consulta una cartomante color di fumo
che le svela il suo prossimo futuro.
Sta per giungere l'uomo di nobile prosapia,
l'invincibile eroe ch'ella attendeva.
È questione di poco, di minuti, di attimi,
presto si sentirà lo zoccolìo dei suoi cavalli
e poi qualcuno busserà alla porta ...
                                        ma
qui il mio occhio si stanca e si distoglie
dal buco della serratura. Ho visto già troppo
e il nastro temporale si ravvolge in se stesso.
Chi ha operato il miracolo è una spugna di birra,
o tale parve, e il suo sodale è l'ultimo
Cavaliere di grazia della Cristianità.
. . . .
ma ora
se mi rileggo penso che solo l'inidentità
regge il mondo, lo crea e lo distrugge
per poi rifarlo sempre più spettrale
e inconoscibile. Resta lo spiraglio
del quasi fotografico pittore ad ammonirci
che se qualcosa fu non c'è distanza

It's not always—almost never—that our self-identity
coincides with our era as measured by instruments.
The large chamber is decorated with baroque stuccoes,
and a window in the background shows a golden park
in Styria where a little mist is burning off in the sun.
The interior is pure Vermeer: smaller and more real
than reality, yet painted with indestructible enamels.
On the left, a small girl dressed as a page
with lace and embroidery right down to her knees
plays with her beloved stuffed animal, a monkey.
To the right, her older sister, Arabella, consults
a fortune-teller who is the color of smoke
and reveals what is to happen in the near future.
A man of noble extraction will be arriving shortly,
the invincible hero for whom she has been waiting.
It won't be long now, a matter of minutes, of instants:
soon the hoofbeats of his horses will be heard,
and then someone will knock at the door ...

                                        but
at this point my eye grows tired and I turn away
from the keyhole. I've seen too much already
and the ribbon of time is winding back on itself.
The one who worked this miracle is a beer-soaked sot,
or so he appears, and his boon companion
some Christian order's last remaining knight.
. . . .
but now
that I reread this, I think only an absence
of identity rules the world, creates it and destroys it
and makes it over again as something more ghostly
and unknowable. What's left is the keyhole view
afforded by this almost photographic painter
to admonish us that if anything ever existed then

tra il millennio e l'istante, tra chi apparve
e non apparve, tra chi visse e chi
non giunse al fuoco del suo cannocchiale. È poco
e forse è tutto.

there's no space at all between a thousand years past and the present moment, between the ones depicted and the ones who weren't, those who saw and those who never managed to focus their lens. It's not much, but maybe it's all there is.

Other Poems (1980)

(Altri Versi)

"...CUPOLE DI FOGLIAME DA CUI SPRIZZA"

Verso Tellaro

... cupole di fogliame da cui sprizza
una polifonia di limoni e di arance
e il velo evanescente di una spuma,
di una cipria di mare che nessun piede
d'uomo ha toccato o sembra, ma purtroppo
il treno accelera ...

"QUEL BISCHERO DEL MERLO È ARRIVATO TARDI"

Notiziaro ore 9 a.m.

Quel bischero del merlo è arrivato tardi.
I piccioni hanno già mangiato tutto.

"L'INVERNO SI PROLUNGA, IL SOLE ADOPERA"

L'inverno si prolunga, il sole adopera
il contagocce. Non è strano che noi
padroni e forse inventori dell'universo
per comprenderne un'acca dobbiamo affidarci
ai ciarlatani e aruspici che funghiscono ovunque?
Pare evidente che i Numi
comincino a essere stanchi dei presunti
loro figli o pupilli.
Anche più chiaro che Dei o semidei
si siano a loro volta licenziati
dai loro padroni, se mai n'ebbero.
Ma ...

"...LEAFY CUPOLAS FROM WHICH A POLYPHONY"

On the way to Tellaro

... leafy cupolas from which a polyphony
of lemons and oranges bursts forth
and the evanescent veil of foam
on a powdery beach it seems
no man's foot has touched, but alas
the train picks up speed ...

"THAT IDIOT BLACKBIRD SHOWED UP LATE"

News bulletin at 9 AM

That idiot blackbird showed up late.
The pigeons already ate everything.

"WINTER DRAGS ON, THE SUN IS USING"

Winter drags on, the sun is using
an eyedropper. Isn't it strange that we,
masters and perhaps inventors of the universe,
in order to comprehend the least thing about it
must entrust ourselves to charlatans and haruspicators
who spring up like mushrooms everywhere?
It seems evident that the Numinous Beings
have begun to tire of the presumptions
of their children or pupils.
Clearer still that God or the semi-deities
have been in their turn discharged
by their own masters, if they ever had them.
But ...

LE PULCI

Non hai mai avuto una pulce
che mescolando il suo sangue
col tuo
abbia composto un frappé
che ci assicuri l'immortalità?
Così avvenne nell'aureo Seicento.
Ma oggi nell'età del tempo pieno
si è immortali per meno
anche se il tempo si raccorcia e i secoli
non sono che piume al vento.

PROSA PER A.M.

Forse si fu chiamati per lo spettacolo
ma l'attesa fu lunga e a cose fatte
rincasando nel gelo e rimbucandoci
là dove uscimmo per il nostro turno
si è incerti se tra il tutto e il nulla pesi
onesta e necessaria la bilancia.

Retrocedendo ed avanzando siamo
al tempo in cui la dolce Anne More
non resse all'undicesima gravidanza.
In tali casi sono male spesi
i curricula pronti per siffatte emergenze.
Resta il mistero perché tanto sangue
e inchiostro non poterono alla fine
rendere degustabile il cacciucco.
Fors'è per fare nascere la Poesia
e l'Averno con lei?
Tra l'orrore e il ridicolo il passo è un nulla.

THE FLEAS

Did you ever have a flea
that combined its blood
with yours
and mixed up a milkshake
to guarantee us immortality?
That's what happened in the Golden Age
of the sixteen hundreds, but today
in the age of full-time professionals
it takes less to get immortalized,
even if time contracts and the centuries
are nothing but feathers on the wind.

PROSE FOR A.M.

Maybe it was our turn for the performance
but the drama was long and when it was over
walking home through the frost to the hole
we had emerged from for our subscription night
we couldn't tell if, in weighing up All and Nothing,
honesty had any heft or scales were necessary.

Going back, or moving forward, we arrive
at the era in which sweet Anne More
couldn't survive her eleventh pregnancy.
In these cases the first-aid protocols invented
for such emergencies are a useless expense.
There remains the mystery of why so much blood
and ink could not in the end produce
a more palatable stew. Maybe
it's so both Poetry and an Entrance
to Hell might be born because of her?
The step from the horrible to the absurd
is no distance at all.

MOTIVI

Forse non era inutile
tanta fatica
tanto dolore.
E forse pensa
così di noi e di sé
questo pseudo merlo orientale
che fischia nella sua gabbia
e imita la nostra voce.
C'è chi fischia di più
e c'è chi fischia di meno
ma anche questo è umano.

◆ ◆ ◆

Costrette a una sola le sue punte
l'aragosta s'imbuca dove non si esce.
Per l'uomo non è questione di assottigliarsi.
O dentro o fuori non saprà mai che farsi.

◆ ◆ ◆

Può darsi che sia ora di tirare
i remi in barca per il noioso evento.
Ma perché fu sprecato tanto tempo
quando era prevedibile il risultato?

◆ ◆ ◆

Quando il fischio del pipistrello
sarà la tromba del Giudizio
chi ne darà notizia agli invischiati
nel Grande Affare?
Saremo a corto di comunicazioni,
in dubbio se malvivi vivi o morti.

MOTIFS

Perhaps it wasn't useless
all the effort
all the pain
And maybe that's what it thinks
about us, about itself,
this pseudo eastern blackbird
that whistles in its cage
and imitates our voice.
There are those who whistle more
and those who whistle less
but that's human too.

◆ ◆ ◆

Its armor reduced to a tip of its shell, the lobster
withdraws into a hole where it can't be extracted.
For a man, it's not a matter of shrinking for safety.
Inside or out, he never knows what to do with himself.

◆ ◆ ◆

It may be that now is the moment to tug
on the oars and make for the boring event.
But why was so much time wasted
when the end was entirely foreseeable?

◆ ◆ ◆

When the squeaking of a bat
becomes the trumpet for the Last Judgment
who will give the news to those of us mired
in the birdlime of the Grand Affair?
We'll be short on information, lowlifes
unsure if we've been captured alive or dead.

APPUNTI

I.

A caccia

C'è chi tira a pallini
e c'è chi spara a palla.
L'importante è far fuori
l'angelica farfalla.

II.

Può darsi

Può darsi che il visibile sia nato
da una bagarre di spiriti inferociti.
Ma tempo e spazio erano già creati?
Peccato, dice Crono al suo collega.
Si stava molto meglio disoccupati.

"AMICI, NON CREDETE AGLI ANNI-LUCE"

Amici, non credete agli anni-luce
al tempo e allo spazio curvo o piatto.
La verità è nelle nostre mani
ma è inafferrabile e sguiscia come un'anguilla.
Neppure i morti l'hanno mai compresa
per non ricadere tra i viventi, là
dove tutto è difficile, tutto è inutile.

"IL BIG BANG DOVETTE PRODURRE"

Il big bang dovette produrre
un rombo spaventoso
e anche inaudito perché non esistevano orecchie.
Queste giunsero solo
dopo molti milioni di millenni.
Verità indiscutibile

CRITICAL NOTES

I.

Hunting

Some fire buckshot
and some shoot bullets.
What's important is to bump off
the angelic butterfly.

II.

It Might Be

It might be that the visible was born
out of a brawl between furious spirits.
But were time and space already created?
A shame, says Cronos to his colleague.
We were much better off unemployed.

"FRIENDS, PUT NO FAITH IN LIGHT-YEARS"

Friends, put no faith in light-years
in time and space, curved or planar.
The truth lies in our hands
but can't be caught and wriggles like an eel.
Not even the dead have ever grasped it,
who don't wish to descend again among the living,
where all is difficult, all is useless.

"THE BIG BANG MUST HAVE PRODUCED"

The Big Bang must have produced
a terrifying roar
albeit unheard, since ears didn't exist.
Those arrived only
after many millions of millennia.
An indisputable truth

che ci riempie di letizia
fatta eccezione per te mia capinera
che avevi stretto col tempo
un patto d'inimicizia
e l'hai rispettato perché forse
ne valeva la pena – chi può dirlo?

A ZIG ZAG

Mi sono allungato sulla sabbia e rifletto.
Leggo la prosa di un Coboldo prete
d'assalto. Ma il pensiero va lontano.
Finito da due secoli il Concilio di Costanza
un pari d'Inghilterra poeta e puttaniere
ormai in punto di morte
negò recisamente la vita eterna e poi
per fare cosa grata al suo confessore
si convertì, ordinò alla moglie
di convertirsi, lei già sconvertita
passando ad altra confessione
e avrebbe convertito senza risparmio
presenti e assenti pur di farla finita.

Ora il sole sta veramente calando.
In fondo il buon Coboldo non ha tutti i torti.
Oggi non ci si ammazza più tra plausi e festeggiamenti.
Si sono scelti altri modi. Esistono 120
confessioni cristiane e pare che siano poche.

RIMUGINANDO
I.

Probabilmente
sta calando la sera. Non per gli anni

that fills us all with joy
with the exception of you, my little blackcap,
who have reached a hostile truce with time
and kept your side of the bargain, perhaps
because it was worth the trouble—
who can say?

ZIGGING AND ZAGGING

Stretched out on the sand, I reflect.
I'm reading the prose of one Kobold, polemical
priest. But my thoughts fly far away.
Two centuries after the Council of Constance,
a peer of England, poet and whoremonger,
by then on the point of death
succinctly denied the life eternal and then
as a gracious favor to his priestly confessor
agreed to convert, commanding his wife
to convert as well (she an apostate moved
on to another confession), and with no compunction
would have ordered the conversion of anyone
present or absent, just to be done with it.

Now the sun is really on the way down.
At heart, good Kobold was not entirely wrong.
Nowadays we don't massacre amid festivals and applause.
We've chosen other methods. There exist 120
Christian denominations, and evidently that's too few.

RUMINATING

I.

Probably
evening is falling. Not due to the years,

che sono molti ma perché lo spettacolo
annoiava gli attori più che il pubblico.
Non mi sono addentrato nella selva
né ho consultato San Bonaventura come C.
che Dio la protegga.
Non si tarda ad apprendere che gli anni
sono battibaleni e che il passato
è già il futuro. E il guaio è che l'incomprensibile
è la sola ragione che ci sostiene.
Se si fa chiaro che le Cause Prime
già contenevano in sé lo scoppio del ridicolo
si dovrà pure cercare altrove senza successo
perché l'avvenire è già passato da un pezzo.

II.

Pare assodato che la vita sia nata
da una furente incompatibilità
di vapori e di gas e questo ci conforta
perché il cervello umano n'esce illeso.
L'infinito, il sublime e altri cacumi
se sono a nostro carico non ci caricano
di un ben fondato orgoglio. Non possumus.
Ma se n'esce incolpevoli. Le colpe
verranno dopo e sono incontestabili.
È il peccato d'orgoglio che dovrebbe
essere perdonato qualora un giudice
fosse a disposizione il che si nega
da più parti. E se poi così non fosse?

OGGI

C'è qualcosa che squassa
che scoperchia e distrugge. Un punto perso da
Chi non vuole soccombere al Nemico.

which are many by now, but because the show
has been boring the actors more than the audience.
I never penetrated the thickets
or consulted Saint Bonaventure like C.,
may God protect her.
It doesn't take long to grasp that the years
go by in a flash and that the past was once
the future. And the trouble is that the incomprehensible
is the only thing that sustains us.
If it's clear that the Primary Causes
contained the explosion of the absurd from the start
then one must search elsewhere and fruitlessly,
since what is to come has already been over for a while.

II.

It seems firmly established that life was born
out of a violent reaction of incompatible
vapors and gas, and this is a comfort to us
since it lets the human brain get off scot-free.
The infinite, the sublime, and other such apogees
may exist at our expense, but they don't burden us
with any cause for pride. *Non possumus.*
From those one gets away guiltless. The guilt
comes later and is indisputable.
It's the sin of pride that needs
to be pardoned insofar as a judge
is available, though the need is denied
by many. And what if that wasn't the case?

TODAY

Something there is that shakes us,
that exposes and destroys. A detail missed by
Those who don't wish to give in to the Adversary.

Purtroppo noi poveri uomini siamo com'è
l'uccello in gabbia al volo degli storni.
Le nostre colpe saranno punite a colpi di scopa.
Non siamo che comparse, in gergo teatrale
utilités.
          A questo punto il poeta
lasciò la penna d'oca con la quale
componeva il poema Il ratto d'Europa
e si guardò allo specchio. Era lui,
era un altro, un demonio, un cerretano?
Forse l'Eco d'Europa, agenzia di encomiastici
soffietti, gli giocava un brutto tiro?
Poi si fece coraggio e riprese il Ratto
buttato nel cestino. D'altra parte
accanto a lui non c'erano animali
che fossero un doppione di se stesso.

NELL'ATTESA

Stiamo attendendo che si apra
la prima delle sette porte.
Era inutile mettersi decorazioni
dal collo fino al plastrone
perché l'attesa durerà un tempo
addirittura esponenziale.
Era inutile mettersi l'abito a doppia coda,
era inutile attendersi sinfonie di salmi
presentat arm di demoni forcuti
cerimonie o frustate, antipasti o cocktails di veleni.
Questa è la prima porta, non ha nessuna voglia
di aprirsi ma richiede un'etichetta.
Non era una follia parlare di porta stretta.
Le porte sono sprangate e a doppio lucchetto.
Forse qualcuno è riuscito a varcarle.

Alas, we unfortunate humans are like
a caged bird when starlings take wing.
Our faults will be punished with swats of a broom.
We're nothing but bit players, in theater jargon
"utilities."
                    At this point the poet
laid aside the quill pen with which
he was composing the poem "The Rape of Europa"
and looked at himself in the mirror. Was it he?
Someone else? A demon? Some charlatan?
Or maybe Europa-Echo, an agency for encomiastic
puff-pieces, was playing him a nasty trick?
Then he took courage and retrieved the "Rape"
he had tossed in the scrap basket. After all,
besides him there weren't any animals
that were doubles of themselves.

WHILE WE WAIT

We're waiting for it to open,
the first of the seven gates.
It was useless to don decorations
from our necks down to our starched shirts
because the waiting will last
a truly exponential amount of time.
It was useless to dress in tails,
useless to attend oratorios of the psalms,
the "present arms" of pitchfork-wielding demons,
ceremonies or beatings, canapés or poison cocktails.
This is the first gate, it has no desire
to open but etiquette insists.
It wasn't foolish to speak of the gate as narrow.
The doors are barred and double locked.
Maybe someone did succeed in crossing the threshold.

Ma era un uomo di *allora*, quando non esistevano
le parole che abbiamo.

L'ALLEVAMENTO

Siamo stati allevati come polli
nel Forward Institute
non quali anatre selvatiche o aquilotti
come chiedeva il nostro
immaginario destino.
E abbiamo annuito in coro intonando la marcia
En avant Fanfan-la-Tulipe!

Così
giusto è morire per una ingiusta causa.
Chi chiedesse una pausa
nella morìa sarebbe un traditore.
Ed è qui che il ridicolo si mescola
all'orrore.

IPOTESI II

Pare
non debba dirsi Italia ma
lo Sfascio.
È un fatto che si allunga, urge studiarlo
finché si esiste, dopo sarà tardi.
Il tempo stesso ne sarebbe offeso;
mancando lo sfasciabile che cosa
potrebbe offrirci? È un tema che va messo
all'ordine del giorno.

But he was a man of *then*, back when they didn't exist,
the words that we have now.

NURSERY

We were raised like chickens
at the Forward Institute
rather than the wild ducks or eaglets
proper to the destiny
we imagined for ourselves.
And we nodded as one while intoning the march
"En avant Fanfan-la-Tulipe!"

Thus
is it just to die for an unjust cause.
Anyone who might ask for a pause
in the slaughter would be a traitor.
And here's where the ridiculous blends
with horror.

HYPOTHESIS II

Apparently
one shouldn't say "Italy" but rather
"the Dismantled."
The fact has ramifications and demands study
so long as it obtains, afterwards will be too late.
Time itself would take offense at this;
lacking a thing to destroy, what else
could it offer us? An item for discussion
to include in the day's agenda.

Come si restringe l'orizzonte
a un certo punto.
Dove sono andati i vasti acquari
in cui si sguazzava
come il pesce nell'acqua senza il sospetto
della lenza e dell'amo.
                    La felicità
sarebbe assaporare l'inesistenza
pur essendo viventi neppure colti dal dubbio
di una fine possibile.
Dice un sapiente (non tutti sono d'accordo)
che la vita quaggiù fosse del tutto improbabile
col corollario (aggiungo) che non era
nient'affatto opportuna. Molti eventi
confortano la glossa. La sconfortano
piccoli *faits divers*; magari il volo
di una formica mai studiata o neppure vista
dagli entomologi.

La buccia della Terra è più sottile
di quella d'una mela se vogliamo supporre
che il mondo materiale non sia pura illusione.
Tuttavia in questo nulla, ammesso che sia tale,
siamo incastrati fino al collo. Dicono
i pessimisti che l'incastro include
tutto che abbiamo creato per surrogare i Dei.
Ma la sostituzione non fu feconda
affermano i fedeli del vecchio Dio.
Forse verrà Egli stesso dicono
a strapparci dal magma e a farsi vivo.

"HOW THE HORIZON SHRINKS"

How the horizon shrinks
at a certain point.
Where have they gone, the vast aquariums
in which we splashed about
like fish in water without the least suspicion
of the hook and line?
                    Happiness
would be savoring non-existence
even while alive and suffering no apprehensions
about a possible ending.
One wise man says (not all of them agree)
that life here on earth was entirely unlikely,
with the corollary (added by me) that it was
in no way opportune. Many incidents
confirm this observation. In contradiction
are a few small *faits divers*; maybe just the flight
of a winged ant, one never studied or so much
as noticed by the entomologists.

"THE CRUST OF THIS EARTH IS THINNER"

The crust of this earth is thinner
than the skin of an apple, if we wish to suppose
the material world is not simply an illusion.
Yet in this nothingness, assuming that's what it is,
we are mired right up to our necks. The pessimists
say the mire includes
all we have invented as a surrogate for the Gods.
But the replacement has yielded no fruit
insist those faithful to the old-time God.
Maybe He Himself will come, they say,
to drag us out of the hot goo and show His face.

Siamo e viviamo dunque una doppia vita
sebbene l'egolatra ne vorrebbe una sola.

O madre Terra o cielo dei Celesti
questo è il guaio
che ci fa più infelici dell'uccello
nel paretaio.

L'ALLEGORIA

Il senso del costrutto non è chiaro
neppure per coloro che riguarda.
Noi siamo i comprimari, i souffleurs nelle buche
ma i fili del racconto sono in mano d'altri.
Si tratta chiaramente di un'allegoria
che dura da un'infinità di secoli supponendo
che il tempo esista oppure non sia parte
di una divina o no macchinazione.
Alcuni suggeriscono marchingegni
che facciano crollare il tutto su se stesso.
Ma tu non credi a questo: la gioia del farnetico
è affare d'altri.

VINCA IL PEGGIORE

disse Colui del quale non può dirsi il nome
ma poi fu preso dal dubbio
e il suo diktat lasciò aperto qualche buco.
Il vincitore il vinto
il vivo il morto l'asino e il sapiente
stanno a contatto di gomito
anzi non stanno affatto
o sono in altro luogo
che la parola rifiuta.

Thus, we exist while living a double life
even if we egomaniacs would prefer a single one.

O Mother Earth, O Celestial Ones of heaven,
this is the predicament
that makes us more miserable than a bird
entangled in a net.

THE ALLEGORY

The meaning of the plot is unclear
even to those whom it concerns.
We're just supporting actors, prompters in the pit,
but the story line is in the hands of others.
Clearly we're dealing with an allegory
lasting an infinitude of centuries, assuming
that time exists, or rather that it is not part
of some great machination, divine or otherwise.
There are those who posit thingamajigs causing
the whole of everything to collapse into itself.
But you don't believe this. The rapture of lunatics
is somebody else's business.

MAY THE WORST MAN WIN

said He Whose Name Must Not Be Spoken
but then he was seized by doubt
and his diktat left open some loopholes.
The victor and the vanquished
the living and the dead the jackass and the sage
stand elbow to elbow
or rather they don't stand at all
unless they're in some other place
that words refuse to name.

"CON QUALE VOLUTTÀ"

Con quale voluttà
hanno smascherato il Nulla.
C'è stata un'eccezione però:
le loro cattedre.
Et tout le reste c'est du charabia
disse taluno; necessario anche questo
per ottenere il resto.

"UNA ZUFFA DI GALLI INFEROCITI"

Una zuffa di galli inferociti
quella di casa nostra?
La differenza è
che colui che di tutto tiene i fili
non si accorge di niente
mentre l'applauso a questi spennamenti
è furente.

"NON È CRUDELE COME IL PASSERO DI VALÉRY"

Non è crudele come il passero di Valéry
l'uccellino che viene a beccar poche briciole
quando s'alza o dirada qualche stecca
l'avvolgibile.

Anche per noi è questione di passaggi,
sia di sopra o di sotto. E le analogie
non si fermano qui. Fino a che punto
lo dicano i filosofi o i maestri
di bricolage fortunatamente
inascoltati è da vedersi.

"WITH WHAT VOLUPTUOUS DELIGHT"

With what voluptuous delight
have they unmasked the Void.
There was an exception, however:
their appointed chairs.
Et tout le reste c'est du charabia
said some; but this was necessary, too,
in order to get everything else.

"A SCUFFLE OF ANGRY CHICKENS"

A scuffle of angry chickens,
is that what we've got here at home?
The difference is
that the guy pulling the puppet strings
isn't aware of a thing,
whereas the applause as the feathers fly
is furious.

"IT ISN'T CRUEL LIKE VALÉRY'S SPARROW"

It isn't cruel like Valéry's sparrow,
the little bird who comes to peck a few crumbs
when one adjusts a slat or raises
the blinds.

For us as well, it's a question of moving on,
be it going up or going down. And the analogies
don't end there. How far they hold
remains to be seen say the philosophers
or do-it-yourself professors,
fortunately ignored.

"L'AVVENIRE È GIÀ PASSATO DA UN PEZZO"

L'avvenire è già passato da un pezzo.
Può darsi però che ammetta qualche replica
dato l'aumento delle prenotazioni.
Con un palmo di naso resteranno
gli abbonati alle prime; e col sospetto
che tutto involgarisce a tutto spiano.

"IL GRANDE SCOPPIO INIZIALE"

Il grande scoppio iniziale
non dette origine a nulla di concreto.
Una spruzzaglia di pianeti e stelle,
qualche fiammifero acceso nell'eterno buio?
L'Artefice supremo era a corto di argomenti?
C'è chi lo pensa e non lo dice,
c'è chi pensa che il pensiero non esiste.
E che più? Forse l'Artefice pensa
che gli abbiamo giocato un brutto tiro.

"È PROBABILE CHE IO POSSA DIRE IO"

È probabile che io possa dire io
con conoscenza di causa
sebbene non possa escludersi che un ciottolo,
una pigna cadutami sulla testa
o il topo che ha messo casa nel solaio
non abbiano ad abundantiam quel sentimento
che fu chiamato autocoscienza. È strano
però che l'uomo spenda miracoli d'intelligenza
per fare che sia del tutto inutile
l'individuo, una macchina che vuole

"THE FUTURE HAS BEEN OVER FOR A WHILE"

The future has been over for a while.
A repeat performance may be allowed, however,
given the increase in advance ticket sales.
What a let-down for the opening-night subscribers,
who are left with the sneaking suspicion
it will all be relentlessly vulgarized.

"THE GIGANTIC INITIAL EXPLOSION"

The gigantic initial explosion
didn't give birth to anything concrete.
A scattering of planets and stars,
a few lit matches in eternal darkness?
Was the Grand Artificer at a loss for a motive?
There are those who think so and don't say it
and those who think thought itself doesn't exist.
And what else? Maybe the Artificer thinks
we played him a nasty trick.

"PROBABLY I CAN SAY THE WORD 'I'"

Probably I can say the word "I"
with some knowledge of the facts,
even if one cannot ignore that a pebble
or a pine cone fallen on my head
or the mouse that has set up house in the attic
does not possess *ad abundantium* that feeling
which we call self-consciousness. It's strange,
though, that Man expends prodigies of intellect
in order to arrange matters so that the individual
has no function whatsoever, imagining a machine

cancellando ogni traccia del suo autore.
Questo è il traguardo e che nessuno pensi
ai vecchi tempi (se mai fosse possibile!).

TEMPO E TEMPI II

Da quando il tempo-spazio non è più
due parole diverse per una sola entità
pare non abbia più senso la parola esistere.
C'era un *lui* con un peso, un suono, forse un'anima
e un destino eventuale, chissà come.
Ora bisogna sentirselo dire: tu sei tu
in qualche rara eccezione perché per distinguersi
occorre un altro, uno che con sottile artifizio
supponiamo diverso, altro da noi, uno scandalo!
Si presume che in fatto di velocità il corvo
(e anche d'intelligenza) possa dare dei punti
all'uomo. È un fatto discutibile. Ma
intanto lui vola con ali sue mentre tu
che della vita sapesti solo l'alba e tu
che lottando col buio avesti migliore destino
e il povero poeta (?) che ti disse
prenotami magari un posto di loggione
lassù se mi vedrai, abbiamo avuto il sospetto
di stringere qualcosa tra le dita.

Per quanto tempo? Ah sì, c'è sempre la malefica
invenzione del tempo!

L'OBOE

Talvolta il Demiurgo, spalla di Dio e Viceré quaggiù,
rimugina su quali macchinazioni
gli attribuiscano i suoi nemici,

that eliminates any trace of its maker.
This is an end-point nobody dreamed of
in the old days (if it was ever possible!).

TIME AND TIMES II

Ever since "space/time" ceased to be
two separate words for a single thing
it seems the word "exist" has lost its meaning.
The term *he* once had a weight, a sound, maybe a soul
and eventual destiny, though who knows what.
Now we have to hear it said: you are you
and a rare exception, since distinguishing the self
requires another, someone who by a cunning trick
we suppose is different, unlike us, what a scandal!
It is to be presumed that in the matter of velocity
(and also of intelligence), a crow could give a few pointers
to a man. It's a debatable issue. But
the bottom line is he flies with his wings while you
who knew only the dawn of a life, and you
who struggled in darkness to achieve a better destiny,
and also the poor poet (?) who says
just save me a seat in the balcony if you
see me up there, all of us have had the suspicion
we grasp at something slipping though our fingers.

For how long? Ah yes, there's always the malevolent
invention of time!

THE OBOE

Sometimes the Demiurge, God's straight man
and his Viceroy down here, mulls over
all the machinations his enemies,

i fedeli al suo Dio perché quaggiù
non giungono gazzette e non si sa
che siano occhi e orecchie. Io sono al massimo
l'oboe che dà il *la* agli altri strumenti
ma quel che accade dopo può essere l'inferno.
Un giorno forse potrò vedere anch'io,
oggi possente e cieco, il mio padrone
e nemico ma penso che prima si dovrà inventare
una cosa da nulla, il Tempo, in cui
i miei supposti sudditi si credano sommersi.

Ma, riflette il Demiurgo, chissà fino a quando
darò la mano (o un filo) al mio tiranno? Lui stesso
non ha deciso ancora e l'oboe stonicchia.

LO SPETTACOLO

Il suggeritore giù nella sua nicchia
s'impappinò di certo in qualche battuta
e l'Autore era in viaggio e non si curava
dell'ultimo copione contestato
sin da allora e da chi? Resta un problema.
Se si trattò di un fiasco la questione
è ancora aperta e tale resterà.
Esiste certo chi ne sa più di noi
ma non parla; se aprisse bocca sapremmo
che tutte le battaglie sono eguali
per chi ha occhi chiusi e ovatta negli orecchi.

"COLUI CHE ALLESTÌ ALLA MENO PEGGIO"

Colui che allestì alla meno peggio
il cabaret
tutto aveva previsto gloria e infamia

God's faithful, ascribe to him, since down here
no information arrives and who knows
if eyes or ears exist. I am at most
the oboe that gives the tuning note to the orchestra,
though what happens after may constitute hell.
Someday perhaps I'll see him, too
(right now I'm powerful yet blind), my master
and adversary, but I think it will first require the invention
of Time, that nothingness in which
my supposed subjects believe themselves immersed.

But, reflects the Demiurge, who knows for how long
I'll be giving a hand (or giving trouble) to my tyrant? He himself
is still undecided, and the oboe is out of tune.

THE PERFORMANCE

The prompter down in his box
no doubt stumbled over some of the witticisms,
and the Author was elsewhere and paid no attention
to the final script, its text in dispute ever since,
and who is it really by? That's still a problem.
It's an open question whether we are dealing
with a fiasco, and a question it will remain.
Clearly someone exists who knows more than we
but says nothing; if he opened his mouth we'd learn
that all battles are the same for those
with their ears plugged and their eyes closed.

"DID THE GUY WHO STAGED THIS CABARET"

Did the guy who staged this cabaret
in the least bad way possible
foresee it all, the glory and the infamy,

o cadde in una trappola
di cui fu prima vittima se stesso?
Che possa uscirne presto o tardi è dubbio.
È la domanda che dobbiamo porci
uomini e porci, con desideri opposti.

"SE L'UNIVERSO NACQUE"

Se l'universo nacque
da una zuffa di gas
zuffa non zuppa allora
com'è possibile, come ...
ma qui gli cadde di mano
quella penna di cigno
che seppure in ritardo
si addice ancora a un bardo.

"SI PUÒ ESSERE A DESTRA"

Si può essere a destra
o a sinistra
o nel centro
o in tutt'e tre, che non guasta.
Ma tutto ciò presuppone
che l'Essere sia certo,
sia la buridda di cui ci nutriamo
quando sediamo a tavola.
Alas, poor Yorick, che teste di cavolo
noi siamo (e questa resta
la nostra sola certezza).

or did he fall into a trap
of which he himself was the first victim?
Whether he'll ever escape is doubtful.
It's the question we pigs and humans
must ask ourselves, torn by opposing desires.

"IF THE UNIVERSE WAS BORN"

If the universe was born
from a puff of gas
a puff not a soup, then how ...
but here the hand lets drop
the quill pen taken from a swan
which, albeit anachronistically,
is thought suitable to a poet.

"ONE MAY BE ON THE RIGHT"

One may be on the right
or on the left
or in the center,
or all three together, which does no harm.
But all of it presupposes
that the Divine Being exists for certain
and is the stew on which we feed
when we sit down to the table.
Alas, poor Yorick, what numbskulls
we are (and this is still
the only certainty for us all).

GIOVIANA

Si scrivono miliardi di poesie
sulla terra ma in Giove è ben diverso.
Neppure una se ne scrive. E certo
la scienza dei gioviani è altra cosa.
Che cosa sia non si sa. È assodato
che la parola uomo lassù desta
ilarità.

"QUANDO IL MIO NOME APPARVE IN QUASI TUTTI I GIORNALI"

Quando il mio nome apparve in quasi tutti i giornali
una gazzetta francese avanzò l'ipotesi
che non fossi mai esistito.
Non mancarono rapide smentite.
Ma la falsa notizia era la più vera.
La mia esistenza fisica risultò un doppione,
un falso come quella planetaria
gode il discusso onore di questi anni.
Sarebbero dunque falsari gli astronomi o piuttosto
falsettanti? La musica vocale
abbisogna di questo o di simili trucchi.
Ma che dire del suono delle Sfere?
E che del falso, del vero o del pot pourri?
Non è compito nostro sbrogliare la matassa.
D'altronde anche filosofi e teologi
sono viventi in carne ed ossa. Ed ecco
il fabbisogno, il dovere di battere la grancassa.

IN ORIENTE

Forse divago dalla retta via.
Questa biforcazione tra Sunna e Scia
non distrugge il mio sonno ma fa di me l'alunno.

JUPITERIAN

Billions of poems are written
on Earth, but on Jupiter it's different.
Not even one gets written. Clearly
the learning of Jupiterians is other than ours.
What it might be is not known. What's sure
is that up there the word "human" provokes
hilarity.

"WHEN MY NAME APPEARED IN ALMOST ALL THE PAPERS"

When my name appeared in almost all the papers
a French gazette advanced the hypothesis
that I had never existed.
Rapid denials were not lacking.
But the false news was the truest.
My physical form had become a sort of double:
it was an illusion like a planetary twin
who enjoyed the public honors of recent years.
So should the star-watchers be called falsifiers
or falsetto artists? Operatic music
requires this and other such artifice.
But what to say about the Music of the Spheres?
And what of the false or the true, or the *potpourri*
of the two? It's not our job to unsnarl the skein.
Besides, even philosophers and theologians
are creatures of flesh and blood. And there it is,
the requirement, the need to beat the big drum.

IN THE ORIENT

Perhaps I stray from the proper path.
This division into Sunni and Shiite
doesn't ruin my sleep, but it gives me cause to study.

È come fare entrare lo spago in una cruna
d'ago.

ALL'ALBA

Lo scrittore suppone (e del poeta
non si parli nemmeno)
che morto lui le sue opere
lo rendano immortale.
L'ipotesi non è peregrina,
ve la do per quel che vale.
Nulla di simile penso nel beccafico
che consuma il suo breakfast giù nell'orto.
Egli è certo di vivere; il filosofo
che vive a pianterreno
ha invece più di un dubbio. Il mondo può
fare a meno di tutto, anche di sé.

MONOLOGO

Non mi affaccio più
dal parapetto
per vedere se arriva
la diligenza a cavalli
che porta gli scolari dai Barnabiti.
Poi lunghi tratti di vita
appaiono scancellati
mi sembra sciocco chi crede
che la vita non soffre interruzioni
non si tratta di morte e resurrezioni
ma di lunghe discese agl'Inferi dove ribolle
qualche cosa non giunta al punto di rottura
ma questo sarebbe la morte che detestiamo

It's like trying to thread a rope through the eye
of a needle.

AT FIRST LIGHT

The writer presumes (and about the poet
we won't even speak)
that once he is dead his works
will render him immortal.
This hypothesis is not unusual,
and I offer it to you for what it's worth.
Nothing of the sort concerns the figpecker
I think, eating his breakfast in the garden below.
He knows he's alive; the philosopher
who lives on the ground floor,
on the other hand, has his doubts. The world
can do without any of it, even without him.

MONOLOGUE

I don't lean out anymore
over the balcony railing
to see if the horse-drawn
carriage has arrived t0 transport
scholars to the Barnabite school.
After that, long periods of my life
seem to have been blotted out
anyone is an idiot who believes
life suffers no interruptions
we're not talking death and resurrections
but of long descents to the Infernal Regions
where something is bubbling
that hasn't quite boiled over
but must be the mortality we all detest

così ci contentiamo di un ribollìo
che è come un tuono lontano,
qualcosa sta accadendo nell'Universo
una ricerca di se stesso
di un senso per poi ricominciare
e noi a rimorchio, cascami
che si buttano via
o cade ciascuno da sé.

ALUNNA DELLE MUSE

Riempi il tuo bauletto
dei tuoi carmina sacra o profana
bimba mia
e gettalo in una corrente
che lo porti lontano e poi lo lasci
imprigionato e mezzo scoperchiato
tra il pietrisco. Può darsi che taluno
ne tragga in salvo qualche foglio, forse
il peggiore e che importa? Il palato,
il gusto degli Dei sarà diverso
dal nostro e non è detto che sia il migliore.
Quello che importa è che dal bulicame
s'affacci qualche cosa che ci dica
non mi conosci, non ti conosco; eppure
abbiamo avuto in sorte la divina follìa
di essere qui e non là, vivi o sedicenti
tali, bambina mia. E ora parti
e non sia troppo chiuso il tuo bagaglio.

that's why we're happy to let it simmer
it seems like thunder in the distance
something is happening in the Universe
something is in search of itself
looking for a way to start up again
and drag us off behind it, pieces
of trash to be tossed aside
or left to collapse on our own.

TO A MUSE IN TRAINING

Stuff your little suitcase
with songs, sacred or profane,
my baby girl
and launch it on the waters,
that the stream may take it far away and then
leave it embedded and half sprung open
in the mire. Possibly some individual
will extract a page to save it, maybe
the worst one, but what matter? The palate,
the taste, of the Gods is likely different
from our own, and it's no sure thing it's better.
What's important is that from the boiling current
some essence emerges to tell us:
you don't know me, I don't know you. And yet
we've been fated to the divine madness
of existing here and not there, alive, my child,
or telling ourselves as much. Now go,
and may your bag be not too tightly closed.

ALL'AMICO PEA

Quando Leopoldo Fregoli udì il passo della morte
indossò la marsina, si mise un fiore all'occhiello
e ordinò al cameriere servite il pranzo.
Così mi disse Pea della fine di un uomo che molto ammirava.
Un'altra volta mi parlò di un inverno a Sarzana
e di tutto il ghiaccio di quell'esilio
con una stoica indifferenza che mascherava la pietà.
Pietà per tutto, per gli uomini, un po' meno per sé.
Lo conoscevo da trent'anni o più, come impresario
come scalpellatore di parole e di uomini.
Pare che oggi tutti lo abbiano dimenticato
e che la notizia in qualche modo sia giunta fino a lui,
senza turbarlo. Sta prendendo appunti
per dirci cosa è oltre le nubi,
oltre l'azzurro, oltre il ciarpame del mondo
in cui per buona grazia siamo stati buttati.
Poche note su un taccuino che nessun editore
potrà mai pubblicare; sarà letto forse
in un congresso di demoni e di dèi
del quale si ignora la data perché non è nel tempo.

NIXON A ROMA

In numero ristretto, setacciati
ma anche esposti a sassaiole e insulti
siamo invitati al banchetto
per l'Ospite gradito. Cravatta nera e niente
code e decorazioni. Non serve spazzolare
sciarpe e ciarpame. Saremo in pochi eletti
sotto i flash, menzionati dai giornali
del pomeriggio che nessuna legge.
Avremo i Corazzieri, un porporato,

TO MY FRIEND PEA

When Leopold Fregoli heard the footsteps of death
he dressed in his morning suit and placed a flower
in his buttonhole and ordered the servants to serve lunch.
That's what Pea told me about the end of a man he admired a lot.
Another time he spoke of a winter in Sarzana
and all the icy weather of that exile,
speaking with a stoic indifference that masked his pity
for everything, for human kind, a bit less for himself.
I knew him for thirty years or more, as an impresario,
as a shaper of words and of men.
It seems these days he's been forgotten
by everyone, as even he may have heard, although
the news wouldn't upset him. He's busy taking notes
in order to inform us of what's beyond the clouds,
beyond the sky, beyond the trash heap of this world
on which we've been discarded by good grace.
A few words jotted in a notebook no editor
will ever publish; it will be read, perhaps,
at a convention of gods and demons
on a date that cannot be known
since it will not exist in time.

NIXON IN ROME

In restricted numbers, carefully chosen,
and yet liable to be insulted, even stoned,
we are invited to the banquet
for the Welcome Guest. Black tie, but no
tails or decorations. No point in polishing
shoes and stuff. We will be the select few
in front of the flash bulbs and mentioned
in the afternoon papers nobody reads.
We are to have an Honor Guard, a cardinal,

le già Eccellenze e i massimi garanti
della Costituzione,
il consommè allo Sherry, il salmone, gli asparagi
da prender con le molle, il Roederer brut,
i discorsi, gli interpreti, l'orchestra
che suonerà la Rapsodia in blu
e per chiudere Jommelli e Boccherini.
Il cuoco è stato assunto per concorso
e per lui solo forse siamo all'Epifania
di un Nuovo Corso.
L'Ospite è giunto; alcuni
negano che sia stato sostituito.
Gli invitati non sembrano gli stessi.
Può darsi che il banchetto sia differito. Ma
ai toast sorgiamo in piedi coi bicchieri
e ci guardiamo in volto. Se i Briganti
di Offenbach non si sono seduti ai nostri posti
tutto sembra normale. Lo dice il direttore
dei servizi speciali.

CÀFFARO

La vecchia strada in salita è via Càffaro.
In questa strada si stampava il Càffaro,
il giornale più ricco di necrologi economici.
Aperto in rare occasioni c'era un teatro già illustre
e anche qualche negozio di commestibili.
Mio padre era il solo lettore del Càffaro
quello dov'era dolce spengersi tra le braccia
d'infinite propaggini. Fornito di monocolo
col nastro il Direttore del giornale
e anche un suo alter ego con in più una mèche bianca
a cui doveva non poco lustro. Si diceva
che per arrotondare i suoi magri profitti

former ambassadors and judges
of the Constitutional Court,
consommé with sherry, salmon, asparagus
served with silver tongs, Roederer brut,
speeches, interpreters, an orchestra
playing "Rhapsody in Blue"
and ending with Jommelli and Boccherini.
The chef has been hired just for the occasion,
and he might be the only one for whom
it's the Revelation of a New Way Forward.
The Guest arrives; a few deny
we've been given a replacement.
The attendees don't seem themselves.
Possibly the banquet has been put off, but
when toasts are made we rise to our feet and raise
our glasses and look each other in the face.
So long as Offenbach's brigands aren't in our places,
everything looks normal. That's what the head
of the Secret Service says.

CÀFFARO

The old uphill street is named Via Càffaro.
It's the street where *Il Càffaro* was printed,
a newspaper rich in cheap obituaries.
There was a theater, too, once well known
but by then open only on rare occasions,
and also a few stores that sold groceries.
My father was our sole reader of *Il Càffaro*,
the one in whose arms its infinite distinctions
died a sweet death. The paper's Senior Editor
had a monocle on a ribbon plus an alter ego
with a curl of white hair that glistened with oil.
It was said that to round out his meager profits

il dotto traduttore del Càffaro annalista
doveva essere lui ma poi l'impresa
passò ad altri e nessuno se ne dolse.
Col fiato grosso salivo a Circonvallazione.
Io con manuali scolastici, il Direttore scendeva
ma il suo occhio di vetro mai si fermò su me.
Di lui nulla si seppe. Più sconsigliato invece
il traduttore mancato portò sulla piccola scena
un suo drammone storico del quale in robone ducale
fu interprete l'Andò e andò malissimo
tanto che quando apparve la nota mèche al proscenio
un grido di bulicciu! divallò dalle alture
e fu l'unico omaggio che i suoi fedeli
se mai ne fu taluno vollero tributargli.

AL GIARDINO D'ITALIA

Larbaud

C'incontrammo al Giardino d'Italia
un caffè da gran tempo scomparso.
Si discuteva la parola romance
la più difficile a pronunziarsi, la sola
che distingue il gentleman dal buzzurro.
Poi ordinò un ponce all'italiana
e la sua dizione era alquanto bigarrée
(ma è un eufemismo).
Vedevo in lui Lotario che battendo
di porta in porta ricerca la sua Mignon.
Per ritrovarla poi, mentre la mia
era perduta.

the learned translator of the *Càffaro Annals*
was he himself, though later when the task
was assigned to another no one complained.
Out of breath, textbooks in hand, I used to climb
up to the boulevard as the Editor came down,
but his glassy eye never fixed its lens on me.
You never heard gossip about him. Less discreet,
however, the translator *manqué* brought to the little
theater stage one of his overwrought historical
dramas in which Flavio Andò donned flowing robes
to play the part of a duke, and it went very badly,
so badly that when that well-known spit curl
appeared at the proscenium arch to take a bow
someone up in the high seats screamed out "faggot!"
and that was the only homage that his fans,
if he ever had any, were willing to bestow.

AT THE GIARDINO D'ITALIA

Larbaud

We met at the Giardino D'Italia,
a café that's been closed a long time.
Romance languages were discussed,
the most difficult to pronounce and the only way
to distinguish a gentleman from a chimney sweep.
Then he ordered a rum punch *"all'italiana,"*
and his diction was somewhat colorful
(but that's a euphemism).
He seemed to me like Lothario, pounding
on doors in search of his Mignon ...
to find her again at last, whereas mine
was lost forever.

"SONO PASSATI TRENT'ANNI, FORSE QUARANTA"

a Charles Singleton

Sono passati trent'anni, forse quaranta.
In un teatro-baracca si riesumava
una noiosa farsa dell'aureo Cinquecento.
Ne comprendevo assai poco ma tutto il resto
era per me decifrato da un provvido amico straniero
che poi scomparve. Lo aveva già visto al Caffè
degli scacchisti. Allora non sapevo
che non esistono rebus per il Patròlogo
ma un nome solo sfaccettato anche se unico.
C'è chi vorrebbe sopprimere anche quello.
Forse doveva essere l'opinione
del misterioso personaggio che ora si rifà vivo
perché ricorda la sera del baraccone
ed il soccorso datomi. Del suo commercio coi Padri
non fece cenno. Sarebbe stato ridicolo.

LE PIANTE GRASSE

Un mio lontano parente era collezionista
di piante grasse. Venivano da ogni parte
per vederle. Venne anche il celebrato (?)
de Lollis delibatore di poesia prosastica.
Si erano conosciuti al Monterosa
ristorante per celibi ora scomparso.
Oggi non esistono più
le serre le piante grasse e i visitatori
e nemmeno il giardino dove si vedevano
simili mirabilia. Quanto al parente
è come non sia esistito mai. Aveva studiato
a Zurigo respinto in ogni materia
ma quando nel nostro paese le cose volgevano al peggio
crollava la testa e diceva eh a Zurigo a Zurigo ...

"THIRTY YEARS HAVE PASSED, MAYBE FORTY"

to Charles Singleton

Thirty years have passed, maybe forty.
In a barn of a theater, they had exhumed
a dull farce from the Golden Age of 1500s drama.
I didn't understand much of it, but what I missed
was deciphered for me by a well-met foreign friend
who later vanished. I'd seen him before
at the chessplayers' café. Back then I didn't know
that no enigmas exist for a specialist in patristics,
there are only the many facets of the unitary Word.
Some would like to eliminate even that division.
This was possibly the point of view
of the mysterious character who now turns up
again so that I might recall that cavernous theater
and the help provided. Of his doings with Church Fathers
he gave no hint. It would have been absurd.

SUCCULENTS

A distant relative of mine was a collector
of succulents. People came from all over
to see them. Even the celebrated (?) de Lollis
came, that great gourmand of prosy poetry.
The two had met at Monterosa, a restaurant
frequented by bachelors that's now long gone.
Today none of it remains,
the greenhouses, the plants, the visitors,
not even the garden where other such marvels
were on display. As for the relative,
it's as if he never existed. He had studied
in Zurich, where he failed every subject,
but whenever things took a bad turn in our town
he'd shake his head and say, "Ah, in Zurich, in Zurich."

Non so che senso abbia il ridicolo
nel tutto/nulla in cui viviamo ma
deve averne uno e forse non il peggiore.

SCHIAPPINO

Il figlio del nostro fattore
aveva fama di pessimo tiratore:
lo chiamavano Schiappa o con più grazia
Schiappino.
Un giorno si appostò davanti alla roccia
dove abitava il tasso in una buca.
Per essere sicuro del suo tiro
sovrappose al mirino una mollica di pane.
A notte alta il tasso tentò di uscire
e Schiappino sparò ma il tasso fece
palla di sé e arrotolato sparve
nella vicina proda. Non si vedeva a un passo.
Solo un tenue bagliore sulla Palmaria.
Forse qualcuno tentava di accendere la pipa.

UNA VISITATRICE

Quando spuntava in fondo al viale
la zia di Pietrasanta noi ragazzi
correvamo a nasconderci in soffitta.
Il suo peccato: era vecchia e noiosa,
una tara che anche ai giovani di allora
pareva incomprensibile, insultante.
Mio padre l'abbracciava, dava ascolto
al fiume di disgrazie in cui la vecchiarda
nuotava come un pesce e poi faceva
scivolare due scudi nel borsetto

I don't know what significance absurdity has
in the all-yet-nothing in which we live, but
it must have a meaning, and maybe not the worst.

KID DUFFER

The son of our estate manager
was known as a terrible shot:
folks called him Duffer, or to be a bit nicer,
Kid Duffer.
One day he set up across from some rocks
where a badger had its den.
To be sure not to miss,
he put breadcrumbs down where he planned to aim.
In the dark of night, the badger tried coming out
and Kid Duffer fired, but the badger
curled up in a ball and rolled away
and disappeared into the river bank nearby.
You couldn't see your hand in front of your face.
Just a faint glow out on Palmaria.
Maybe someone was trying to light his pipe.

A FEMALE VISITOR

When she came into sight at the end of the street,
our aunt from Pietrasanta, we kids
would run off to hide in the attic.
Her sin: she was old and boring,
shortcomings that even the youth of that era
found incomprehensible and offensive.
My father would give her a hug and listen
to the torrent of complaint in which the old crone
swam like a fish, and then he'd slip
a couple of coins into the handbag

sempre aperto di lei. E infine le diceva
affréttati, tra poco arriverà
il trenino 'operaio' che serve a te.
Non l'ho mai vista; oggi avrebbe assai più
di cento anni. Eppure quando leggo o ascolto
il nome PIETRASANTA penso ai pochi scudi,
al dolore del mondo, alla ventura-sventura
di avere un avo, di essere trisnipote
di chissà chi, di chi non fu mai vivo.

I NASCONDIGLI II

I.

Il canneto dove andavo a nascondermi
era lambito dal mare quando le onde erano lunghe
e solo la spuma entrava a spruzzi e sprazzi
in quella prova di prima e dopo il diluvio.
Larve girini insetti scatole scoperchiate
e persino la visita frequente (una stagione intera)
di una gallina con una sola zampa.
Le canne inastavano nella stagione giusta
i loro rossi pennacchi; oltre il muro dell'orto
si udiva qualche volta il canto flautato
del passero solitario come disse il poeta
ma era la variante color cenere
di un merlo che non ha mai (così pensavo)
il becco giallo ma in compenso esprime
un tema che più tardi riascoltai
dalle labbra gentili di una Manon in fuga.
Non era il flauto di una gallina zoppa
o di altro uccello ferito da un cacciatore?
Neppure allora mi posi la domanda
anche se una rastrelliera di casa mia
esibiva un fucile così detto a bachetta,

she always left open. And at last he'd tell her
"Hurry up, you'll miss your commuter train."
I never went to see her; today she'd be well over
a hundred. And yet whenever I read or hear
the name PIETRASANTA I think of the few coins,
of the woe of this world, of the fortune/misfortune
of having an ancestor, of being the great grandnephew
of who knows who, of someone who was never alive.

HIDING PLACES II

I.

The canebrake where I used to go hide as a child
was lapped by the sea when the waves were long rollers
and it was only the spray that splashed up to spatter me
in that rehearsal for a before-and-after of the Flood.
Larvae, tadpoles, insects, open cans and cartons,
and even the regular appearance (for a whole season)
of a hen that was missing a foot.
The canes, when the time was right, raised
red pennants up their poles; beyond the garden wall
you could sometimes hear the warbled song
of "the solitary sparrow," as the poet says,
though it was in fact just the gray variation
of a blackbird that never (so I used to think)
possessed a golden beak but in recompense
fluted out a motif I would hear again later
from the genteel lips of a Manon in flight.
Was the quavering really made by the lame hen
or some other bird winged by a hunter?
At the time I didn't ask myself that question,
even if the gun-rack in my home displayed
what used to be called a pellet rifle, a weapon

un'arma ormai disusata che apparteneva
in altri tempi a uno zio demente.
Solo la voce di Manon, la voce
emergente da un coro di ruffiani,
dopo molti anni poté riportarmi
al canneto sul mare, alla gallina zoppa
e mi fece comprendere che il mondo era mutato
naturalmente in peggio anche se fosse assurdo
rimpiangere o anche solo ricordare
la zampa che mancava a chi nemmeno
se ne accorse e morì nel suo giuncheto
mentre il merlo acquaiolo ripeteva quel canto
che ora si ascolta forse nelle discoteche.

II.

Una luna un po' ingobbita
incendia le rocce di Corniglia.
Il solito uccellino color lavagna
ripete il suo omaggio a Massenet.
Sono le otto, non è l'ora
di andare a letto, bambini?

OTTOBRE DI SANGUE

Nei primi giorni d'ottobre
sulla punta del Mesco
giungevano sfiniti dal lungo viaggio
i colombacci; e fermi al loro posto
con i vecchi fucili ad avancarica
imbottiti di pallettoni
uomini delle mine e pescatori
davano inizio alla strage dei pennuti.
Quasi tutti morivano ma il giorno che ricordo

by now long out of fashion but that belonged
in that earlier era to a crazy uncle.
And yet just the voice of Manon, her aria
rising above a chorus of whores and pimps,
was all it took to take me back after many years
to the canebrake by the sea, to the one-legged hen,
and make me understand the world had changed,
naturally for the worse, even if it was absurd
to feel nostalgia for, absurd even to remember,
the missing claw of a creature who was unaware
of what it lacked and died in its reed-bed
while the seaside blackbird repeated some notes
that these days you might hear in a discotheque.

II.

A moon a little swollen
lights up the cliffs of Corniglia.
A common little bird the color of slate
repeats its homage to Massenet.
It's eight o'clock, children,
isn't it time for bed?

OCTOBER BLOOD

During the first days of October
at Mesco Point
the wood doves arrived completely
exhausted by their long migration;
and waiting for them there
armed with ancient muzzle-loaders
stuffed full of birdshot
the stonecutters and fishermen
began their massacre of feathered creatures.
Almost all were killed, but on the day I remember

uno se ne salvò che già ferito
fu poi portato nel nostro orto.
Poteva forse morire sullo spiedo
come accade a chi lotta con onore
ma un brutto gatto rognoso
si arrampicò fino a lui e ne restò
solo un grumo di sangue becco e artigli.
Passione e sacrifizio anche per un uccello?
Me lo chiedevo allora e anche oggi nel ricordo.
Quanto al Mesco e alla Punta non ne è traccia
nel mio atlante scolastico di sessant'anni fa.

UN INVITO A PRANZO

Le monachelle che sul lago di Tiberiade
reggevano a fatica un grande luccio
destinato dicevano a Sua Santità
mi chiesero di restare qualora il Santo Padre
dichiarasse forfait (il che avvenne dipoi).
Non senza assicurarsi che sebbene at large
io ero un buon cattolico. Purtroppo
generose sorelle sono atteso al monte degli Ulivi
fu la risposta accolta da rimpianti
benedizioni e altro. Così ripresi il viaggio.
Sarebbe stato il primo luccio della mia vita
e l'ho perduto non so se con mio danno
o con vantaggio. Un luccio oppure un laccio?

NEL DUBBIO

Stavo tenendo un discorso
agli 'Amici di Cacania'
sul tema 'La vita è verosimile?'
quando mi ricordai

one dove survived, even though wounded,
and was carried into our vegetable garden.
It might have died honorably on a kitchen spit
pierced like a hero fallen on his sword
but an ugly cat covered with mange
crept up and reached it and all that was left
was some blood and the beak and the claws.
Is there Passion and Sacrifice even for a bird?
I asked myself then, and recollecting I ask it now.
As for Mesco and its Point, there's no trace of them
in my grade-school atlas from sixty years ago.

AN INVITATION TO LUNCH

The little nuns by the Sea of Galilee
had with great effort landed a large pike
destined, they said, for the table of His Holiness,
and they asked me to stay in case the Holy Father
declined his due (as in fact happened after).
Not without reassuring themselves that I,
even if "at large," was a good Catholic. "Alas,
generous sisters, I'm expected at the Mount of Olives"
was my reply, received with many regrets
and blessings and so forth. And so I went my way.
It would have been the first pike of my life,
and I missed out on it, whether to my detriment
or advantage I don't know. A fish or a fish trap?

IN DOUBT

I was addressing a discourse
to the "Friends of Cacania"
on the subject of "Is Life Probable?"
when I remembered

ch'ero del tutto agnostico,
amore e odio in parti uguali e incerto
il risultato, a dosi alternate.
Poi riflettei ch'erano sufficienti
cinque minuti
due e mezzo alla tesi
altrettanti all'antitesi
e questo era il solo omaggio
possibile a un uomo senza qualità.
Parlai esattamente trentacinque secondi.
E quando dissi
che il sì e il no si scambiano le barbe
urla e fischi interruppero il discorso
e mi svegliai. Fu il sogno più laconico
della mia vita, forse il solo non sprovvisto
'di qualità'.

LA GLORIA O QUASI

A Ginevra alle felicemente defunte
Rencontres Internationales c'era una poltrona
sempre vuota e una scritta che diceva
Riservata alla vedova
di Affricano Spir.
Simili scritte appaiono sulle poltrone
di mezzo mondo
come apprendo da fogli autorevoli quali l'Eco
di Mazara del Vallo e il Diario de Pamplona.
Anche per me suppongo dev'essere scattata
tale macchinazione che non risparmia i celibi.
Certo, Affricano, se la sua incredibile
consorte ch'ebbi il vanto di conoscere
lo avesse risparmiato, esulterebbe,
nichilista com'era in senso filosofico e non politico.

I was agnostic regarding all things,
alternately loving and hating in equal measure
and uncertain of the upshot.
Then I reflected that five minutes
would be sufficient,
two and a half for the proposition
and the same for the rebuttal,
and that this was the only homage
possible for a man without qualities.
I spoke for exactly thirty seconds.
And when I said
that "yes" and "no" are inextricably entangled
rude whistles and outcries interrupted my speech
and I woke up. It was the shortest dream
of my life, perhaps the only one not lacking
in "qualities."

GLORY OR SOMETHING LIKE IT

In Geneva at the happily defunct
Rencontres Internationales there was an armchair
left always empty with a plaque that read
"Reserved for the Widow
of Afrikan Spir."
Similar inscriptions appear on chairs
half the world over
as may be gathered from authoritative newspapers
like Mazara del Vallo's *Eco* and Pamplona's *Diario*.
I suppose schemes of that sort will be sprung on me, too,
since old bachelors aren't spared such machinations.
Certainly Afrikan, if his scarcely credible spouse,
whom I had the honor of knowing, had spared him,
would have rejoiced, nihilist that he was
in philosophical matters, though not political ones.

Non riuscì ad annullarsi. Oltre l'impresa
fallimentare della sua consorte
esistono dovunque quei monumentali
libri, le Enciclopedie che alla lettera S
portano un nome che anche senza di loro
e con scarsa sua gioia avrebbe galleggiato
alla meglio sul tempo.

"MI PARE IMPOSSIBILE"

Mi pare impossibile,
mia divina, mio tutto,
che di te resti meno
del fuoco rosso verdognolo
di una lucciola fuori stagione.
La verità è che nemmeno
l'incorporeo
può eguagliare il tuo cielo
e solo i refusi del cosmo
spropositando dicono qualcosa
che ti riguardi.

"NON PIÙ NOTIZIE"

Non più notizie
da San Felice.

Hai sempre amato i viaggi
e alla prima occasione
sei saltata fuori
del tuo cubicolo.

Ma ora come riconoscersi
nell'Etere?

He didn't succeed in becoming nothing himself.
Apart from the ill-fated efforts of his wife,
his monumental tomes are in libraries everywhere,
and encyclopedia volumes bearing the letter "S"
contain a name that, even without them
and of no satisfaction to him, would have managed
to bob on the waters of oblivion.

"IT SEEMS IMPOSSIBLE"

It seems impossible,
my divine one, my everything,
that what remains of you
after the greenish-red flames
is less than a firefly out of season.
The truth is that not even
the incorporeal
is adequate to your heaven
and only the rejects of the cosmos
in their awkward way can say
anything about you.

"NO MORE NEWS"

No more news
from San Felice.

You always loved traveling
and the first chance you got
you leapt out of your niche
in the columbarium.

But now how to recognize ourselves
in the ether?

"TERGI GLI OCCHIALI APPANNATI"

Tergi gli occhiali appannati
se c'è nebbia e fumo nell'aldilà,
e guarda in giro e laggiù se mai accada
ciò che nei tuoi anni scolari fu detto vita.
Anche per noi viventi o sedicenti tali
è difficile credere che siamo intrappolati
in attesa che scatti qualche serratura
che metta a nostro libito l'accesso
a una più spaventevole felicità.
È mezzogiorno, qualcuno col fazzoletto
ci dirà di affrettarci perché la cena è pronta,
la cena o l'antipasto o qualsivoglia mangime,
ma il treno non rallenta per ora la sua corsa.

"IL MIO CRONOMETRO SVIZZERO AVEVA IL VIZIO"

Il mio cronometro svizzero aveva il vizio
di delibare il tempo a modo suo.
E fu così
ch'erano solo le 5 e non le 6
quando potei sedermi al caffè San Marco.
Parve un'inezia, magari una fortuna
questo allungarsi dell'appuntamento
sebbene a lei pesasse assai l'attesa
ma il suo pallore divenne presto il mio.
Quale durata deve avere l'ultimo
(presumibile) addio? Non c'è manuale
di Erotica che illustri degnamente
la scomparsa di un dio. In tali eventi
che il cronometro avanzi o retroceda
non conta nulla.

"WIPE YOUR MISTY EYEGLASSES"

Wipe your misty eyeglasses
if there's fog and smoke in the hereafter
and peer around and look down there to see
if it might actually be happening, the thing
that in your student years was called Life.
It's hard for us too, we the living, or so we say,
to believe we're trapped here and waiting
for some lock to spring and a door to open
that will provide us unrestricted access
to the most terrifying possible bliss.
It's high noon. Soon someone will flag us down
and tell us to hurry because dinner is ready,
dinner or snacks or some sort of food, but
for now our train doesn't slow down at all.

"MY SWISS TIMEPIECE HAD THE VICE"

My Swiss timepiece had the vice
of telling time according to its own ideas.
And that's the reason
it was just 5:00 and not 6:00
when I found a seat in the Café San Marco.
It seemed insignificant, or maybe fortunate,
this stretching out of our appointment,
even if the delay weighed heavily on her,
and yet her pallor soon became my own.
How long should it take, the last
(presumably) goodbye? There exists
no erotic manual that adequately illustrates
the disappearance of a deity. In such cases
a chronometer running fast or slow
counts for nothing at all.

LUNI E ALTRO

1938

Arrestammo la macchina
all'ombra di alcune rovine.
Qui sarà sbarcata la jeunesse dorée
e dopo secoli vi sostò Gabriel
per compiervi la pessima delle sue prove.
Più modesti dobbiamo contentarci
di poco: il Poveromo, la Fossa dell'Abate.
Troppe cose, dicesti. Ne ho abbastanza
di cadaveri illustri.
                    E ripartimmo
senza nessuna nostalgia: quel poco
che ancora oggi resiste.

"HO TANTA FEDE IN TE"

A C.

Ho tanta fede in te
che durerà
(è la sciocchezza che ti dissi un giorno)
finché un lampo d'oltremondo distrugga
quell'immenso cascame in cui viviamo.
Ci troveremo allora in non so che punto
se ha un senso dire punto dove non è spazio
a discutere qualche verso controverso
del divino poema.

So che oltre il visibile e il tangibile
non è vita possibile ma l'oltrevita
è forse l'altra faccia della morte
che portammo rinchiusa in noi per anni e anni.

OF LUNI AND OTHER THINGS

1938

We stopped the car
in the shade of some ruins.
Here's where *la jeunesse dorée* once came ashore
and where centuries later, Gabriel stayed
to undergo the worst of his trials.
Of humbler station, we must content ourselves
with less: with Poveromo and Fossa dell'Abate.
It's too much, you said. I've had enough
of illustrious cadavers.
                              And we went our way
without feeling any nostalgia, which
is what little remains today.

"I HAVE GREAT FAITH IN YOU"

to C.

I have great faith in you
and it will endure
(this the foolishness I told you one day)
until a lightning bolt from another world destroys
the gigantic garbage heap on which we live.
We'll find each other someplace then,
if it makes sense to say that when there is no place,
and talk over some debatable stanza
of the divine poem.

I know that beyond the visible and the tangible
no life is possible, but perhaps the afterlife
is only the other side of the death
we carried inside us for years and years.

Ho tanta fede in me
e l'hai riaccesa tu senza volerlo
senza saperlo perché in ogni rottame
della vita di qui è un trabocchetto
di cui nulla sappiamo ed era forse
in attesa di noi spersi e incapaci
di dargli un senso.

Ho tanta fede che mi brucia; certo
chi mi vedrà dirà è un uomo di cenere
senz'accorgersi ch'era una rinascita.

CLIZIA DICE

Sebbene mezzo secolo sia scorso
potremo facilmente ritrovare
il bovindo nel quale si stette ore
spulciando il monsignore delle pulci.
Sul tetto un usignolo si sgolava
ma non ebbe successo. Quanto al gergo
delle sagre del popolo o a quello
delle commedie o farse vive solo
in tradizioni orali, se con noi fosse
come un giorno un maestro del sermone umile
nonché del bronzeo della patrologia,
tutto sarebbe facile. Ma dove
sarà quel giorno e dove noi?
Se esiste un cielo e in esso molte lingue,
la sua fama d'interprete salirebbe
in altri cerchi ancora e il puzzle sarebbe
peggiore che all'inferno di noi sordomuti.

I have great faith in myself
and you have rekindled it without wishing to
without knowing it because in every fragment
of our life here there is a pitfall
of which we are unaware and which lies
in wait until we are helpless and alone
before it gives the broken piece its meaning.

I have great faith and it burns me. Surely
anyone seeing me would say: "He's a man in ashes,"
unaware it has been a rebirth.

CLIZIA SAYS

Even if half a century has passed,
we could easily find it again,
the bay window where we tarried for hours
picking over subtleties of that poet of fleas.
Up on the roof a nightingale tried to sing
itself hoarse with no success. As for the slang
used in popular festivals or found
in the comedies and farces which now exist
only in oral tradition, if we'd had with us, as once
before, an expert in both the speech of humble sermons
and the ornate phrases used by Fathers of the Church,
everything would have been simple. But where
has that earlier day gone, and where are we?
If a heaven exists and in it many tongues,
his fame as an interpreter may ascend
to yet higher spheres and the puzzlement
be worse than in our inferno of the deaf and dumb.

CLIZIA NEL '34

Sempre allungata
sulla chaise longue
della veranda
che dava sul giardino,
un libro in mano forse già da allora
vite di santi semisconosciuti
e poeti barocchi di scarsa reputazione
non era amore quello
era come oggi e sempre
venerazione.

PREVISIONI

Ci rifugiammo nel giardino (pensile se non sbaglio)
per metterci al riparo dalle fanfaluche
erotiche di un pensionante di fresco arrivo
e tu parlavi delle donne dei poeti
fatte per imbottire illeggibili carmi.
Così sarà di me aggiungesti di sottecchi.
Restai di sasso. Poi dissi dimentichi
che la pallottola ignora chi la spara
e ignora il suo bersaglio.
                              Ma non siamo
disse C. ai baracconi. E poi non credo
che tu abbia armi da fuoco nel tuo bagaglio.

INTERNO/ESTERNO

Quando la realtà si disarticola
(seppure mai ne fu una) e qualche sua parte
s'incrosta su di noi
allora un odore d'etere non di clinica
ci avverte che la catena s'è interrotta

CLIZIA IN '34

Forever stretched out
on the chaise longue
of the terrace
that looked over the garden,
a book in your hand perhaps even then
Lives of some little-known saints
or Baroque poets of small reputation
that wasn't love it was
as it is now and forever
veneration.

PREDICTIONS

We took refuge in the garden (a hanging one
if I'm not mistaken) to escape the erotic
stories of a retiree who had just arrived,
and you spoke of the women whom poets
use to flesh out their unreadable odes.
"That'll be me," you added with a sly glance.
I was struck dumb. Then I said: "You forget
that a bullet doesn't know who shot it
and doesn't know its target."
                              "But we,"
said C., "aren't at a carnival booth. And besides
I don't think you're packing any pistols."

INTERNAL/EXTERNAL

When reality disconnects from itself
(assuming anything was ever real) and part
of it hardens over us like a scab
an ethereal albeit non-pharmaceutical odor
alerts us that the links have separated

e che il ricordo è un pezzo di eternità
che vagola per conto suo
forse in attesa di rintegrarsi in noi.
È perciò che ti vedo
volgerti indietro dall'imbarcadero
del transatlantico che ti riporta
alla Nuova Inghilterra
oppure siamo insieme nella veranda
di 'Annalena'
a spulciare le rime del venerabile
pruriginoso John Donne
messi da parte i deliranti abissi
di Meister Eckart o simili.
Ma ora squilla il telefono e una voce
che stento a riconoscere dice ciao.
Volevo dirtelo, aggiunge, dopo trent'anni.
Il mio nome è Giovanna, fui l'amica di Clizia
e m'imbarcai con lei. Non aggiungo altro
né dico arrivederci che sarebbe ridicolo
per tutti e due.

NEL '38

Si era con pochi amici
nel Dopopalio
e ci fermammo per scattare
le foto d'uso.
Ne ho ancora una, giallo sudicia,
quasi in pezzi,
ma c'è il tuo volto incredibile,
meraviglioso.
Si era nel '38.
Più tardi dissero

and that each memory is a fragment of eternity
wandering about on its own
waiting perhaps to be reunited with us.
And because of this I see you
looking back from the embarkation pier
of the transatlantic liner that is taking you
home again to New England
or else we're together on the terrace
of the Pensione Annalena
picking over the rhymes of that venerable
prurient poet John Donne
having set aside the delirious depths
of Meister Eckhart or some such.
But now my telephone rings and a voice
I struggle to recognize says "Hi."
"I wanted to tell you," it adds, after thirty years.
"My name is Giovanna, I was the friend of Clizia
who sailed with her that time." I don't reply
and I don't say "Until we meet again,"
which would be an absurdity
both for her and for me.

IN '38

It was with a few friends
during the post-Palio celebration
and we stopped to shoot
a few instant photos.
I still have one, yellow and grimy,
almost in shreds,
but there it is, your incredible face,
amazing.
It was in '38.
Later people said

che bordeggiavi 'a sinistra'
ma la notizia non mi sorprese
perché sapevo che l'Essere
non ha opinioni o ne ha molte
a seconda del suo capriccio
e chi non può seguirle
ne è inseguito.
Si era nel '38.

QUARTETTO

In una istantanea ingiallita
di quarant'anni fa
ripescata dal fondo di un cassetto
il tuo volto severo nella sua dolcezza
e il tuo servo d'accanto; e dietro Sbarbaro
briologo e poeta – ed Elena Vivante
signora di noi tutti: qui giunti per vedere
quattro ronzini frustati a sangue
in una piazza-conchiglia
davanti a una folla inferocita.
E il tempo? Quarant'anni ho detto e forse zero.
Non credo al tempo, al big bang, a nulla
che misuri gli eventi in un prima e in un dopo.
Suppongo che a qualcuno, a qualcosa convenga
l'attributo di essente. In quel giorno eri tu.
Ma per quanto, ma come? Ed ecco che rispunta
la nozione esecrabile del tempo.

"POICHÉ LA VITA FUGGE"

Poiché la vita fugge
e chi tenta di ricacciarla indietro
rientra nel gomitolo primigenio

that you cozied up to "the Left"
but the news didn't surprise me
because I knew that the Divine Being
has no opinions or else has a great many
according to pure caprice,
and anyone who can't follow them
will find he's been followed himself.
It was in '38.

QUARTET

In the yellowed instant photo
from forty years ago
fished out of the bottom of a drawer
your severe face in all its sweetness
and your slave alongside; and in the background
Sbarbaro, botanist and poet—and Elena Vivante,
our lady and leader: assembled here to see
four horses whipped until they bled
in a shell-shaped piazza
in front of a crowd gone wild.
And the date? Forty years ago, but maybe none.
I don't believe in time, in the Big Bang, in anything
that divides events according to a before and after.
I suppose the quality of existing is to be attributed
to some one or thing. On that day it was you.
But how and for how long? And it pops up again,
the execrable notion of time.

"SINCE LIFE IS FLEETING"

Since life is fleeting
and those who try to chase after it
return to a primordial confusion,

dove potremo occultare, se tentiamo
con rudimenti o peggio di sopravvivere,
gli oggetti che ci parvero
non peritura parte di noi stessi?
C'era una volta un piccolo scaffale
che viaggiava con Clizia, un ricettacolo
di santi Padri e di poeti equivoci che forse
avesse la virtù di galleggiare
sulla cresta delle onde
quando il diluvio avrà sommerso tutto.
Se non di me almeno qualche briciola
di te dovrebbe vincere l'oblio.

E di me? La speranza è che sia disperso
il visibile e il tempo che gli ha dato
la dubbia prova che questa voce È
(una E maiuscola, la sola lettera
dell'alfabeto che rende possibile
o almeno ipotizzabile l'esistenza).
Poi (sovente hai portato
occhiali affumicati e li hai dimessi
del tutto con le pulci di John Donne)
preparati al gran tuffo.
Fummo felici un giorno, un'ora un attimo
e questo potrà essere distrutto?
C'è chi dice che tutto ricomincia
eguale come copia ma non lo credo
neppure come augurio. L'hai creduto
anche tu? Non esiste a Cuma una sibilla
che lo sappia. E se fosse, nessuno
sarebbe così sciocco da darle ascolto.

where are we to conceal, if we seek
(by stratagems simple or worse) to live on,
those objects which appear to us
to be the part of ourselves worth saving?
Once upon a time, there was a little bookcase
that traveled with Clizia, a small receptacle
of Sainted Fathers and ambiguous poets
that might perhaps have the virtue
of bobbing on the crest of the waves
when the Flood has sunk everything else.
If no part of me, at least some bit
of you ought to triumph over oblivion.

And of me? The hope is that the visible
world may be blown away, along with the time
that gave it the dubious proof my voice Exists
(with a capital E, the only letter
of the alphabet which renders possible,
or at least hypothetical, Existence).
At that point (you often used to wear
dark glasses and you abandoned them
entirely amid the fleas of John Donne)
get ready to take the big plunge.
Were we happy for a day, an hour, an instant,
and can that happiness be destroyed?
There are those who say everything begins again
exactly as it was, but I don't believe it,
not even as a hope. Did you believe
that, too? The Cumaean Sibyl doesn't exist,
so far as I know. And if she did, no one
would be so silly as to listen to her words.

CREDO

1944

Forse per qualche sgarro nella legge
del contrapasso
era possibile che uno sternuto in via Varchi 6 Firenze
potesse giungere fino a Bard College N. J.
Era l'Amore? Non quello che ha popolato
con un orrendo choc il cielo di stelle e pianeti.
Non tale la forza del dio con barba e capelli
che fu detronizzato dai soci del Rotary Club
ma degno di sopravvivere alle loro cabale.
Credo vero il miracolo che tra la vita e la morte
esista un terzo status che ci trovò tra i suoi.
Che un dio (ma con la barba) ti protegga
mia divina. Ed il resto, le fandonie
di cui siamo imbottiti sono meno
che nulla.

A CLAUDIA MUZIO

Eravate sublime
per cuore e accento,
il fuoco e il ghiaccio fusi
quando Qualcuno disse basta
e fu obbedito.
Ovviamente
non fu affar vostro la disubbidienza
ma questo non conforta, anzi infittisce
il mistero: che sia pronto a dissolversi,
ciò che importa, ma tardo e incancellabile
l'essere per cui nascere fu un refuso.

I BELIEVE

1944

Perhaps due to some discrepancy in the law
of action and reaction
it was possible for a sneeze in Florence at 6 Via Varchi
to make it all the way to Bard College, N.J.
A miracle of Love? Not the kind which populated
the skies with stars and planets in a horrendous Bang.
Such magic is beyond the bearded, long-haired god
who was dethroned by the members of the Rotary Club
but remains worth saving from their conspiracy.
Yet I believe the miracle is real, that between life and death
there exists a third condition that claimed us for its own.
May a god (one with a beard) protect you
my divine friend. And for the rest, the nonsense
in which we find ourselves swaddled is less
than nothing.

TO CLAUDIA MUZIO

You were sublime
both for emotion and for diction
fire and ice combined
when Someone said "Enough"
and was obeyed.
Obviously
disobedience was none of your affair
but that's no comfort. In fact, it deepens
the mystery: that it should be ready to vanish
(the key fact), though after some delay and indelible,
this being for whom "being born" was a misprint.

"QUANDO LA CAPINERA"

Quando la capinera fu assunta in cielo
(qualcuno sostiene che il fatto
era scritto nel giorno della sua nascita)
certo non si scordò di provvedersi
di qualche amico del suo repertorio
scelto tra i più fidati, Albert Savarus
e la piccola Alice strappata dal suo Wonderland.
Per il primo non sono problemi
ma per l'altra
distolta dall'ombrello del suo fungo
non mancherà qualche dissidio: ch'io
sappia tra i micologi del cielo
è buio pesto.

CARA AGLI DEI

Vista dal nostro balcone
in un giorno più chiaro d'una perla
la Corsica appariva sospesa in aria.
È dimezzata dicesti come spesso
la vita umana.
Le vieillard s'approcha, il avait
bien cinquante ans
dissi citando Rousseau, non si saprà mai
quanto deve durare una vita. Non sapevo
allora che tu per il tuo conto
avresti risolto il problema
scacciandone una parte: 'un barba!'.
Non so ancora se fui caro o discaro agli Dei
e quale di queste Maschere abbia raggione o torto,
Il avait bien 50 ans! Quello ch'è sottinteso
in quel bien potrebbe anche farmi impazzire.

"WHEN THE BLACKCAP"

When the blackcap was assumed into heaven
(there are those who maintain this event
was written on the day of her birth)
surely she didn't forget to provide herself
with some chosen friends, the most-trusted
among her subjects for song: Albert Savarus
and little Alice torn away from her Wonderland.
Concerning the first there are no difficulties,
but as for the other,
detached from her mushroom umbrella,
perhaps objections will not be lacking: for all
I know the mycologists in heaven
are absolutely benighted.

BELOVED OF THE GODS

Seen from our balcony
on a day of jewel-like clarity
Corsica seemed to float in the sky.
"It's divided into halves," you often said,
"a human life."
*"Le vieillard s'approcha, il avait
bien cinquante ans,"*
I replied, quoting Rousseau, "One can never tell
how long a life will last." I didn't know
then that in your case
you would resolve the problem
by canceling part of it: 'what a bore!'
I still don't know if I was loved or unloved by the Gods
and which of these Masks is or is not justified.
Il avait bien 50 ans! What's implied
in that *'bien'* is enough to drive me crazy.

UNA VISITA

Roma 1922

Quasi a volo trovai una vettura
lasciando l'hôtel Dragoni.
Ci volle non poco tempo per giungere al cancello
dove lei mi attendeva. Dentro erano i parenti
e gl'invitati. Le signore in lungo
gli uomini in nero o nerofumo
io solo in grigio. C'erano due ammiragli
omonomi, il prefetto, due ex ministri
molto loquaci. Si parlò di tutto,
con preferenza per guerre da fare o prendere.
Io e lei quasi muti.
Venne servito il tè coi buccellati
di Cerasomma. E noi sempre meno loquaci.
Dopodiché allegai che fosse per me il tempo
'di togliere il disturbo' e non trovai obiezioni.
Permetti
che ti accompagni disse lei uscendo dal suo mutismo.
Ma era ormai per poco, col cancello vicino.
Sulla ghiaia il suo passo pareva più leggero.
Non tardò una vettura.
                        Hasta la vista dissi
facendomi coraggio. La sua risposta si fuse
con uno schiocco di frusta.

POSTILLA A 'UNA VISITA'

Certo non fu un evento degno di storia
quel primo mio viaggio a Roma. Ma la storia
anche la privatissima storia di Everyman
registra ben altre sciocchezze. Non sa che farsene
di due cuori neppure infranti (e se anche

Rome 1922

Almost on wings, I found a hansom cab
as I left the Hotel Dragoni.
It took some time to drive to the gate
where she was waiting for me. Inside were relatives
and invited guests. The ladies in evening gowns,
the men in black or grayish black,
myself just in gray. There were two admirals
of the same name, the regional magistrate, two
very chatty former politicians. The conversation
touched on everything, with a preference
for war, either given or received.
She and I were almost mute.
Tea was served, along with Christmas cookies
from Cerasomma. And we were less and less talkative.
After that, I pretended it was time
"to remove my intrusion" and encountered no objections.
"Permit me
to accompany you," she said, breaking her silence.
But not for long at that point, with the gate nearby.
On the gravel drive, her step seemed to lighten.
A cab came quickly.
                    "Hasta la vista," I said
gathering my courage. Her reply was lost,
fused with a crack of the whip.

A NOTE ON "A VISIT"

Certainly it wasn't an event worthy of historical
notice, my first trip to Rome. But history,
even the highly personal history of Everyman,
records entirely different stupidities. It doesn't
know what to do with two hearts not even broken

lo fossero o lo furono?). La storia è disumana
anche se qualche sciocco cerca di darle un senso.

AH!

Amavi le screziature le ibridazioni
gli incroci gli animali
di cui potesse dirsi mirabil mostro.
Non so se nel collège di Annecy
qualcuno abbia esclamato vedendoti e parlandoti
con meraviglia Ah! E fu da allora
che persi le tue tracce. Dopo anni seppi
il peggio. Dissi Ah! e tentai di pensare ad altro.
Rari i tuoi libri, la Bibbia
e il Cantico dei Cantici,
un bosco per la tua età
con tanto di cartello cave canem,
qualche romanzo del Far West e nulla
che fosse scritto per l'infanzia e i suoi
confini così incerti. Tuttavia,
se tu fossi scomparsa allora, anche a te
non sarebbe mancato un tenerissimo
Ah!
Ma più tardi nessuno
o soltanto il buon Dio quale che fosse
accompagnò la tua vacanza con un Ah!
che dicesse stupore o smarrimento.
Forse qualcuno si fermò sull'A
che dura meno e risparmia il fiato.
Poi fu silenzio. Ora l'infante là
dove si sopravvive se quella è vita
legge i miei versi zoppicanti, tenta
di ricostruire i nostri volti e incerta dice
Mah?

(and what if they were or were once?). History is inhuman
even if some fools try to give it a meaning.

AH!

You loved variations and hybrids
crossbred animals
one might call marvelous creatures.
I don't know if at the *Collège* in Annecy
someone saw you or spoke to you and said
in amazement "Ah!" And it was then
that I lost track of you. Years later I learned
the worst. I said "Ah!" and tried to think of other things.
You had only a few books. The Bible
with The Song of Songs
(an enchanted wood for one your age
complete with a sign reading *Cave Canem*),
some novels of the Far West, and nothing
intended for childhood or the blurry
boundaries that define it. In any case,
had you disappeared back then, you too
would not have departed without a tender
"Ah!"
Later, though, no one,
or only the Good Lord such as he might be,
reacted to your absence with an "Ah!"
that might express bewilderment or loss.
Maybe somebody stopped at "A,"
which doesn't take as long and saves breath.
And then silence. Now the child up there
where one survives, if that is living,
reads my awkward verses and tries
to reconstruct our faces and says uncertainly
"Wha . . . ?"

FROM

Fugitive Poems (1980)

(Poesie Disperse)

PICCOLO DIARIO

Sono infreddato, tossicchio
è lo strascico dell'influenza,
domani andrò a ricevere
una medaglia per benemerenze
civiche o altre che ignoro.
Verrà a prendermi un tale
di cui non so più il nome. Ha una Mercedes,
presiede un Centro Culturale (quale?).

◆ ◆ ◆

Si accumula la posta
'inevasa' sul tavolo. Parrebbe
che io sia molto importante
ma non l'ho fatto apposta.
Dio mio, se fosse vero
che mai saranno gli altri?

◆ ◆ ◆

Comunicare, comunicazione,
parole che se frugo nei i miei ricordi
di scuola non appaiono. Parole
inventate più tardi,
quando venne a mancare anche il sospetto
dell'oggetto in questione.

LA COMMEDIA

Si discute sulla commedia:
se dev'essere un atto unico o in tre o in cinque
come il genere classico;
se a lieto fine o tragico; se sia

LITTLE DIARY

I've got a cold, a nasty cough
that's left over from a case of the flu;
tomorrow I'm due to receive
a medal for civic merit
or other virtues I know nothing about.
Some guy whose name I can't recall
will come pick me up. He's got a Mercedes,
he's the head of a Cultural Center (which one?).

◆ ◆ ◆

The mail is piling up
"unanswered" on the table. It appears
I've become a very important person,
though I didn't do so on purpose.
My God, if that were true
what would other people be?

◆ ◆ ◆

"To communicate," "communication,"
words I can't find when I search
my schoolboy memories. Words
invented later,
when we no longer had any conception
of the subject being discussed.

THE DRAMA

The drama is under discussion:
should it should consist of one act or three or five,
as in the classical genre, and should
the ending should be happy or tragic;

latitante l'autore o reperibile
o se un'équipe lo abbia destituito;
se il pubblico pagante e gli abusivi,
onorevoli o altro
non stronchino i soppalchi dell'anfiteatro;
se sulla vasta udienza calerà
un sonno eterno o temporaneo; se
la pièce debba esaurire tutti i significati
o nessuno;
si arguisce che gli attori non siano necessari
e tanto meno il pubblico; si farfuglia dai perfidi
che la stessa commedia sia già stata
un bel fiasco e ora manchino i sussidi
per ulteriori repliche; si opina
che il sipario da tempo è già calato senza
che se ne sappia nulla; che il copione
è di un analfabeta ed il sovrintendente
non è iscritto al partito. Così si resta in coda
al botteghino delle prenotazioni
in attesa che lo aprano. O vi appaia
il cartello ESAURITO.

IL DONO

Chi ha il dono dell'umore
può disprezzare la vita?
Questa vita, sia pure, ma non è la sola,
non è la sola vita
dei fatti nostri, delle nostre parole.
E forse non è vita
neppure quella dell'aldilà
secondo la proposta antropomorfica
che dà barba e capelli al pantocratore
e le civetterie del superstar.

is the author in hiding or can he be found,
or did the production crew give him the boot;
will the paying public and all the free entries,
legitimate or otherwise, overload
the nose-bleed seats up in the balcony;
will the huge audience fall
asleep for just a while or for all eternity; and should
the play exhaust every possible meaning
or none whatsoever.
It's argued the actors are unnecessary,
and even more so the audience; there are nasty
rumors that the same piece was staged already
and was a flop, and that there's no money now
for further revivals; some suggest
that the curtain fell on this show a long time ago
without anyone knowing, that the script
was written by an illiterate, that the director
isn't enrolled in the party. So it is one stands
in line at the advance box-office
waiting for it to open. Or else
a sign is posted: SOLD OUT.

THE GIFT

Must anyone having the gift of humor
view this life with disdain?
This life, quite possibly, but it's not
the only one, it's not the sole life
of our actions, of our words.
And maybe that isn't life
either, the one in the Great Beyond
we imagine anthropomorphically
by giving a beard and hair to the Pantocrator
along with the coy behavior of a superstar.

Noi non sappiamo nulla ma è ben certo
che sapere sarebbe dissoluzione
perché la nostra testa non è fatta per questo.
Solo ci è noto che non è sapere
l'escogitazione,
quella che fa di noi i più feroci animali,
ma un dono che ci fu dato
purché non se ne faccia uso
e nemmeno si sappia di possederlo.
Ed è un sapere mutilo, inservibile,
il solo che ci resta nell'attesa
come in sala d'aspetto che giunga il treno.

VANILOQUIO

La scomparsa del mondo che manda al settimo cielo
sinistri questuanti non m'interessa per nulla.
Sembra che sia lontana, per ora non minacciosa.
Inoltre c'è il pericolo che la notizia sia falsa.
Falsa o vera è scomparsa rateale.
E la mia quota? Forse ne ho già pagata
qualche rata e per le altre posso attendere.
'Ma fia l'attender corto'? O maledette
reminiscenze! Mi ostino a conficcare
nel tempo ciò che non è temporale.
Ho incontrato il divino in forme e modi
che ho sottratto al demonico senza sentirmi ladro.
Se una partita è in giuoco io non ne sono l'arbitro
e neppure l'urlante spettatore.
Me ne giunge notizia ma di rado.
Il mio tutore m'ha lasciato in margine
per una sua finezza particolare.
In tempo di carestia sono preziosi gli avanzi.
Non mi lusingo di essere prelibato,

We don't know anything, but it's clear
that if we did it would be our undoing,
since our brains weren't made for this.
All we're certain of is that knowledge
isn't mere cogitation but is a gift
which makes us the fiercest of animals,
although it's bestowed upon us
on the condition it not be used
or even thought of as our own.
And it's a damaged knowledge, inadequate,
the only thing left us while we wait
as if in a departure lounge until the train arrives.

EMPTY TALK

The end of this world that sends to a seventh heaven
evil-looking supplicants doesn't interest me at all.
It seems far off, for the moment no threat.
Besides, there's a danger the news is false.
False or true, it's a disappearance by installments.
And my payment plan? Maybe I've covered
some of the cost already, and for the rest I can wait.
"But the wait will be brief"? O cursed
recollections! I'm stubborn and insist
on belaboring time with what is not temporal.
I've encountered the divine in shapes and ways
I swiped from the demonic, and I didn't think it theft.
If it's a game that's being played, I'm no referee
and no screaming spectator, either.
I do get news of it, though not too often.
My protector left me by the wayside
out of some scruple of his own.
In time of famine even scraps of food are precious.
I don't flatter myself I'm a delicacy,

non penso che l'infinito sia una mangiatoia
ma penso col mio mezzo limitato: il pensiero.
Non si pensa con l'occhio, non si guarda
con la testa. Parrebbe che i nostri sensi
siano male distribuiti. Oppure
è un mio difetto particolare. Meglio
una vita indivisa suddivisa
che un totale impensabile mostruoso;
o forse ...

GLORIA DELLE VITE INUTILI

Siamo così legati al nostro corpo
da non immaginarne la sopravvivenza
che come un fiato, non un flatus vocis,
fatta eccezione per i soprassalti
di un tavolino che una versiera ad hoc
a modo suo manovri per far cassetta.
Ma una trasformazione che non sia
inidentità come può immaginarsi?
Così il grande e ventruto Kapdfer,
tale il nome di guerra benché non legato
a imprese eroiche o erotiche degne di un Margutte,
trent'anni fa un fantasma evanescente
distrutto dalla droga, poi risorto
tutto d'un pezzo non più riconoscibile
per la sublime sua inutilità,
compì il suo capo d'opera morendo
senza lasciare traccia che lo perpetui a lungo.
Chissà che
simili vite siano le sole autentiche,
ma perché, ma per chi? Si batte il capo

and I don't think of the infinite as a slop-trough,
but I'm thinking with limited means: my thought.
You don't think with your eyes, you don't see
with your brains. It could be our faculties
are poorly situated. Or maybe
that's my defect alone. Better
an entire life lived in pieces
than a coherent whole unthinkably grotesque,
or maybe ...

THE GLORY OF USELESS LIVES

We are so attached to our bodies
that we can't even imagine surviving
except as a sort of breath (and no *flatus vocis*),
unless it be in the acrobatics
of a séance table some *ad hoc* medium
manipulates as her way to get money.
But how to imagine a transformation
that isn't an end of identity?
Thus the great and big-bellied Kapdfer
(his *nom di guerre* even if unaccompanied
by heroic deeds or amorous adventures worthy of a Margutte)
thirty years ago became an evanescent ghost
destroyed by drugs only to later reemerge
entirely whole albeit unrecognizable
due to his sublime uselessness
and complete his life's masterpiece by dying
without leaving any trace
that might perpetuate his memory at length.
Who knows if
lives like that aren't the only authentic ones ...
but to what end, and for whom? We beat our heads

contro la biologia come se questa
avesse un senso o un'intenzione; ma
è troppo chiedere.

LA VITA IN PROSA

Il fatto è che la vita non si spiega
né con la biologia
né con la teologia.
La vita è molto lunga
anche quando è corta
come quella della farfalla –
la vita è sempre prodiga
anche quando la terra non produce nulla.
Furibonda è la lotta che si fa
per renderla inutile e impossibile.
Non resta che il pescaggio nell'inconscio
l'ultima farsa del nostro moribondo teatro.
Manderei ai lavori forzati o alla forca
chi la professa o la subisce. È chiaro che l'ignaro
è più che sufficiente per abbuiare il buio.

against biology as if it made sense
or had any purpose; but
that's too much to ask.

LIFE IN PLAIN WORDS

The fact is that life can't be explained
either by biology
or by theology.
Life is extremely long
even when it's short
as a butterfly's—
life remains prodigal
even when this earth produces nothing.
It's frantic, the effort to which one goes
only to render life useless and impossible.
All that's left is fishing around in the subconscious,
the final farce of our moribund theater.
I'd condemn whoever practices or undergoes analysis
to forced labor or the gallows. Clearly such dolts
are more than enough to make the darkness obscure.

The House in Olgiate
and Other Poems (1986)

(La Case di Olgiate e Altre Poesie)

[I] LA CASA DI OLGIATE

In quel tempo era ancora vivo
il piccolo Tonino nella casa
alta sul cavalcavia.
Io la vedevo, la casa, dall'autostrada,
ignorando te e lui: non mi balzava
il cuore come adesso. L'ignoranza
mia occultava l'avvenire, il fil-
di-ferro del domani, là giunti, si troncava.

V'entrai molti anni dopo
(il bimbo era morto da tanto,
susurrando "mi duole per te, mamma"),
conobbi l'orto, il giardiniere, il tuo
boudoir di diciottenne, disammobiliato,
l'impronta appena visibile di un cerchio sul muro – lo specchio – ,
e non potevo parlare. Tra quelle stanze
una parte alitante di te mi bastava.

Il trillo del tuo cardellino più tardi si spense
all'ombra del giglio rosso da me lasciato.
Famelico delle tue tracce mi affaccio su rettangoli
di verze, su cespugli di dalie impolverate,
e il vecchio custode mi segue, più inebetito di me
nei corridoi, nel solaio mentre dal basso giunge
un crepitare isocrono di macchine,
ma non bava d'aria nell'afa.

Così i destini s'annodano, mia tigre, e intanto tu
dietro le lenti affumicate spii
nugoli pigri e sull'Olona putrido
l'efflorescenza dei disinfestanti.
Si snodano i destini. Mai da me intraveduta,
la tua casa friulana ora s'allarga

[I] THE HOUSE IN OLGIATE

At that time he was still alive,
little Tonino, in the house
high above the overpass.
I used to see it from the highway, your home,
though knowing nothing of you or him; my heart
didn't leap the way it does now. My ignorance
hid what was coming; the chain connecting
future days reached that point and snapped.

I got in the place many years later
(the little boy had died long since
murmuring "I feel bad for you, Mama")
to find the vegetable patch, the gardener,
your teenage boudoir emptied of furniture,
a circular mark barely visible on the wall—the mirror—
and I couldn't speak. The mere hint of you
in those rooms was all I could bear.

The trill of your goldfinch would fall silent
in the shadow of the red lily I abandoned.
Hungry for any trace of you, I'm looking now
at the cabbages, the clumps of dusty dahlias,
and the elderly caretaker, more dazed than I,
follows me through the hallways, through the attic,
as a constant sputter of traffic rises from below,
and there's no breath of air in the summer heat.

So do destinies grow linked, my Tigress, while you,
hidden behind your dark glasses, observe
the lazy little clouds and the efflorescence
of pesticides on the putrid stream of the Olona.
Yet destinies diverge. Never so much as glimpsed
by me, now your longed-for Friuli home looms large,

nel desiderio, l'aia dove incontro al futuro
irruppe la tua infanzia, e gia volava.

[II] "NON SO SE QUELLO CHE ANNUSO"

Non so se quello che annuso
sia odore di sangue o di stalla.
È un ricordo di scuola? Caracalla
nominò senatore il suo cavallo.

[III] "E VENNERO DA ULTIMO I DISERBANTI"

E vennero da ultimo i diserbanti ...
Ci scrolliamo di dosso quest'orrenda
pulizia. Anche una pulce
potrebbe confortarsi. Siamo all'osso.

[IV] LA PARATA MILITARE

Il ministro Canazzi si irrigidisce
dinanzi a una bandiera o ad una lapide.
Avrà altro per la testa l'infelice
e in fin dei conti chi glielo fa fare.
E sarà poi davvero così disgraziato?
Credo che chi ha forbito le sue ciarpe
abbia raggiunto il summit, il cacume
del suo epistème, né può chiedere altro.
Ma lui non ne sa nulla e tanto meno
l'eccellente Canazzo. Dopo tutto
chissà chi vorrebbe al suo posto.

that threshing floor where your childhood exploded
into the future and was already flying away.

[II] "I DON'T KNOW IF WHAT I SMELL"

I don't know if what I smell
is the odor of blood or of stables.
Is it a schoolboy memory? Caracalla
made a senator out of his horse.

[III] "AND NOW HERE COME THE HERBICIDES"

And now here come the herbicides ...
We shrug off such horrible
sanitary measures. Even a flea should
be able to take comfort. We're down to the bone.

[IV] THE MILITARY PARADE

The defense minister Canazzi suddenly stiffens
to attention in front of a flag or a tombstone.
The poor guy must have other things on his mind,
and the bottom line is, who can order him to do it?
And is his behavior really so disgraceful?
I think a man who has fussed with his full-dress
uniform has reached the top, the empirical peak
of his understanding, and can't ask for more.
Yet such a man knows nothing, and His Excellency
Canazzo knows even less. And after all,
who knows who would want to be in his place?

[V] NEL CONDOMINIO

1.

Un piccolo gatto nero
è venuto a trovarci due o tre volte.
Nessuno di noi l'ha voluto.
Dopo non s'è più visto,
deve'essersi inselvatichito.
Buon per lui.

2.

E noi poveri diavoli, famelici
di servitù
abbiamo barattato la primogenitura
per un povero piatto di lenticchie.
Incommestibili. Ma sicure.

[VI] "IL CONIUGIO"

Il coniugio
di Marx e Freud è alle porte.
Non più indugi, decidete,
imbrattacarte.

[VII] "DI BUONORA"

Di buonora
vengono i merli sul terrazzo
per beccare qualcosa

poveri merli innocenti
come noi

[V] IN THE APARTMENT BLOCK

1.

A little black cat
came to visit us two or three times.
None of us wanted him.
Then he was no more to be seen,
he must have gone wild.
Good for him.

2.

And we poor devils, starving
for servility,
have bartered our birthright
for a miserable plate of lentils.
Inedible. But a sure thing.

[VI] "THE MARRIAGE"

The marriage
of Marx with Freud is at hand.
No more delay, make up your minds,
you scribblers.

[VII] "AT AN EARLY HOUR"

At an early hour
the blackbirds come to the terrace
to eat a little something

poor blackbirds innocent
like us

[VIII] "MI HANNO MANDATO DALL'IUGOSLAVIA"

Mi hanno mandato dall'Iugoslavia
una corona di similoro
in viaggio ha perduto qualche dente.

[IX] "LA CULTURA AVANZA A PASSI DA GIGANTE"

La cultura avanza a passi da gigante
e in scala macroscopica riproduce
le invasioni barbariche

chi ha figli ha tutto da temere
i figli di questi figli non avranno
più nulla da sapere
nulla da perdere

[X] "PER AVERE SERVITO AGLI AVVENTORI"

Per avere servito agli avventori
salmì di pantegane
Bibe di Ponte all'Asse
che fu già immortalato (fin che dura)
da un mio distico
pare che andrà in galera.

Forse solo per questo il mio nome
galleggerà fino a tarda sera.

[XI] G. PASCOLI

Gli è mancata purtroppo l'autoironia
(la più importante che sia)

[VIII] "THEY SENT ME A CROWN FROM YUGOSLAVIA"

They sent me a crown from Yugoslavia
made out of imitation gold
it lost a few prongs on the way.

[IX] "OUR CULTURE IS ADVANCING WITH GIANT STEPS"

Our culture is advancing with giant steps
and reproducing on a macroscopic scale
the barbarian invasions

anyone with children has everything to fear
the children of those children will have
nothing left to learn
nothing to lose

[X] "FOR HAVING SERVED HIS CUSTOMERS"

For having served his customers
a ragù made from sewer rats
Bibe at Ponte all'Asse
who was immortalized (while it lasts)
in a distich of mine
looks like he'll go to jail.

That could be the only reason my name
might bob on the water late into the evening.

[XI] G. PASCOLI

Alas, he lacked irony regarding himself
(the most important kind there is)

[XII] RARITÀ DEI RAPACI

Molle, arruffata figlia di Minerva
fino a jeri regina, oggi serva.

[XIII] "LA GIUSTIZIA OGGI AVANZA A PASSI VELOCI"

La giustizia oggi avanza a passi veloci;
ma figlia di Minerva non è padrona
ma serva.
Bello è l'intervento, soave lo spintone.

[XIV] "I GIORNI DELL'ANTILOPE FURONO TORMENTOSI"

i giorni dell'antilope furono tormentosi
i giornali ne dettero i connotati
o almeno un attendibile identikit
anche se non fornito di quattro zampe

[XV] IN GIARDINO

Un'intera famiglia di gatti,
madre e figli
si arrampicano sugli alberi, poi ricadono.
Sono le 4.50, il problema è
di arrivare alle 7, 71/2, l'ora
più decente per prendere congedo.
È molto se di tanto in tanto, forse
per dieci minuti appena la vita può apparire
com'è, come non è, meravigliosa.
Ma più frequenti lo +++, m'accasciano con le domande
sul mio modo di vedere, di pensare.
E non posso rispondere Signori
non esisto, non sono mai esistito

[XII] RARITY OF THE RAPTORS

Soft, fluffy daughter of Minerva,
a queen until yesterday, a servant today.

[XIII] "JUSTICE THESE DAYS MOVES AT A RAPID PACE"

Justice these days moves at a rapid pace;
yet the daughter of Minerva is no longer in charge
but a servant instead.
It's a slick operation, and the shove was gentle.

[XIV] "THE DAYS OF THE ANTELOPE WERE TORMENTED"

the days of the antelope were tormented
the newspapers provided the facial features
or at any rate offered a reliable identikit
even if it wasn't equipped with four legs

[XV] IN THE GARDEN

An entire family of cats,
mother and kittens
climbed into the trees, then fell back down.
It's 4:50, the problem is
how to arrive at 7, or half-past 7, the hour
when it's polite to take one's leave.
It's a lot if from time to time, maybe
for just ten minutes, life appears
as it is, or as it isn't, marvelous.
But more often [I'm blind to] it; they plague me with questions
about my way of seeing, my way of thinking.
And I can't give them the answer: "Sirs,
I don't exist, I have never existed,

e questa è la sola certezza.
                        Ma è impossibile.

[XVIA] "LA VITA È COME UN SIGARO"

La vita è come un sigaro
che si fuma da sé
quando è acceso e deposto nel cendrier.

A volte pare spengersi
poi si riattizza di colpo
e allora l'anno il secolo il millennio
parole che hanno un senso
per noi, non per chi fa
che il sigaro fumi se stesso
fumi
fumi …

[XVIB] "COME UN SIGARO AVANA"

Come un sigaro avana
la terra si fuma da sé
ma sul piattino resta la cenere.

Per ora la cenere siamo noi
ma la seconda legge della termodinamica
ci assicura
che non è mai troppo presto
per farsi vedere
non è mai troppi tardi
per congedarsi.

and this is the only certainty."
                                    But it's impossible.

[XVIA] "LIFE IS LIKE A CIGAR"

Life is like a cigar
that smolders by itself
when it's lit and left in an ashtray

Sometimes it seems to go out
then suddenly it flares up again
and hence "year" "century" "millennium"
words that have meaning
for us, not for whoever makes
the cigar smolder on by itself
smoldering
smoldering...

[XVIB] "LIKE A HAVANA CIGAR"

Like a Havana cigar,
this world keeps smoldering on
though the ashes rest in the tray.

For now, the ashes are us,
but the second law of thermodynamics
assures us
that it's never too early
to show up
and it's never too late
to depart.

[XVIC] "MA SE ESISTESSE UN AVANA"

Ma se esistesse un avana
che non tira o tira a metà?
In questo caso si dovrebbe scegliere
tra la gioia e l'orrore.

[XVII] DA UNA FINESTRA SUL GIARDINO

Ai primi lucori dell'alba sento fischiare il merlo.
Non finirà sullo spiedo come accade ai tordi.
Ma il tordo zirla, il merlo gorgheggia a tutto spiano.
La loro vita mi sembra inutile, la mia lo parrà a questi pennuti.
Ma quale utilità avrà la vita del cosmo?
Non sarebbe stato più ragionevole farne a meno?
Il guaio è che per pensare così bisogna esistere.
Così il cerchio si chiude maledettamente.
E intanto esistono i fisici, i cosmologi
gli onniscienti
e persino i cristiani da 2000 anni soltanto
e suddivisi in non so quante fazioni e frazioni.
Ultima beffa il marxo-leninismo
e siamo così serviti di barba e di parrucca.

[XVIII] DIETRO FRONT

Venne a pranzo Ezra
e c'era un pollo arrosto.
Amo la cossia disse
e fu servito.

Ritornò a pranzo Ezra
e nel menu ancora il pollo.
Odio la cossia disse
e fu servito.

[XVIC] "BUT IF A CIGAR EXISTED"

But if a cigar existed
that had no draw or drew poorly?
In that case one would have to choose
between joy and horror.

[XVII] FROM A GARDEN WINDOW

At the first glimmer of dawn I hear the blackbird whistle.
He won't wind up on a spit the way thrushes do.
Yet a thrush trills softly, a blackbird warbles full blast.
Their lives seem useless to me, but to these feathered creatures
mine must seem the same. Of what use is the life of the cosmos?
Wouldn't it have made more sense to do without it?
The trouble is that to think this way one must exist.
Thus our wretched circular reasoning closes on itself.
And meanwhile there exist physicists, cosmologists,
the omniscient ones,
and also the Christians of a mere 2000 years,
plus the subdivisions of who knows how many factions and sects.
The latest joke is Marxist-Leninism,
and so are we waited on both hand and foot.

[XVIII] ABOUT-FACE

Ezra came to lunch
and there was roast chicken.
I adore the thigh meat he said
and was served accordingly.

Ezra came back to lunch
and chicken was still on the menu.
I loathe the thigh meat he said
and was served accordingly.

Che cosa sono in confronto
i dietro front militari?

[XIX] "NESSUNO HA MAI VISTO IN VISO"

Nessuno ha mai visto in viso
la morte.
Solo si sa che sia
scomparsa e putrefazione.

Il mio cagnuolo Galiffa
è morto da sessant'anni
ora saltella felice
nello'orto del suo paradiso.

[XX] "CAMMINO IN GALLOZOPPO"

Cammino in gallozoppo
come si dice di una gallina
che ha perduto una zampa
ma saltella qua e là.
Sono entrato nel canneto
che è fronteggiato dal mare
per lungo tratto
e vi ricerco larve
vermi abbozzi di vita
tutto ciò che rimase
del crac esistenziale
che in noi continua a sopravvivere
a occhi chiusi
perché la natura è avara
di occhi a chi più ne abbisogna.

Compared to this, what
are military about-faces?

[XIX] "NO ONE HAS EVER LOOKED DEATH"

No one has ever looked death
in the face.
All one hears is it might be
disappearance and putrefaction.

My little dog Galiffa
has been dead for sixty years
now he bounds happily
in the garden of his paradise.

[XX] "I'M WALKING CHICKEN-HOBBLE"

I'm walking chicken-hobble
as they say of a hen
that's missing a claw
and hops about here and there.
I've entered the canebrake
that for a long stretch
faces the sea
and I search there for grubs
worms traces of life
all that remains
of the existential cataclysm
which continues to live on in us
when we close our eyes
because nature is stingy with eyes
for those who need them most.

[XXI] "USCIMMO SUL BOW WINDOW O QUALCOSA DI SIMILE"

Uscimmo sul bow window o qualcosa di simile
(il mio inglese è imperfetto) per liquidare
l'impiegato di banca che vantava le sue conquiste.
"Io sono una di quelle che s'incontrano nei versi
dei sedicenti poeti. Così sarà di me".
Scartai l'ipotesi con orrore. Eppure quella sera
eri più intelligente di me. Senza contare
che mai il proiettile
si riconosce nel bersaglio.

[XXII] "TEMPO E SPAZIO DUE CASE"

Tempo e spazio due case
inabitabili eppure
abitate perché
sono una sola se anche
c'è chi crede che una
sia più che superflua.

[XXIII] "È UNO SPROPOSITO CREDERE"

È uno sproposito credere
che il ricordo sia immateriale.
Provate a condurmi
al Biffi Scala
e sarà un fuggi fuggi generale
o meglio nessuno si muoverà
perché ci sono due modi di vedere
l'invisibile
e il modo giusto sarebbe il mio
se fossi certo di esistere,
perché è un miracolo se sono riuscito
a farlo credere.

[XXI] "WE WENT OVER TO THE 'BOW WINDOW' OR SOME SUCH"

We went over to the 'bow window' or some such
(my English is imperfect) to rid ourselves
of the bank clerk who was boasting of his conquests.
"I'm one of those women who turns up in the verse
of self-styled poets. It will be like that with me."
I rejected the suggestion with horror. And yet you
were smarter than I that afternoon. Not to mention
that the bullet
never knows its target.

[XXII] "TIME AND SPACE, TWO UNLIVABLE ... "

Time and space, two unlivable
houses, and yet
they're inhabited because
they're actually one and the same
even if some people think
one by itself is more than superfluous.

[XXIII] "IT'S A MISTAKE TO BELIEVE"

It's a mistake to believe
that memory has no substance.
Try taking me
to Biffi Scala
and it might cause a complete stampede
or better yet no one will lift a finger
because there are two ways of seeing
the invisible
and the right way would be mine
if I was certain of my existence,
since it's a miracle if I've succeeded
in making others believe it at all.

[XXIV] "DELL'UNIVERSO, LA CITTÀ DI DIO"

Dell'universo, la città di Dio
conosciamo ben poco.
La cottura fu tarda,
a lenta fuoco.

Ora per alcuni asini
siamo all'accelerazione,
quella che pare preludere quasi
a una totale estinzione.

Resterà forse il pensiero,
senza colui che lo pensa.
Resta la pura follia,
il buco nero, L'Enciclopedia
dello zero.

[XXV] "DOPO L'INVENZIONE DEL MOTORE A SCOPPIO"

Dopo l'invenzione del motore a scoppio
la vita vale il doppio o il triplo? è una questione
che nessuno si pone – et pour cause.

[XXVI] "SIAMO IMPRIGIONATI IN UN'ALLEGORIA"

Siamo imprigionati in un allegoria,
che sarà decifrata da esseri non umani.
Non dirmi Clizia che questo è pessimismo.
La palla del fucile non sa dove è diretta.

[XXVII] "SI PARLA E STRAPARLA"

Si parla e straparla
dei buchi neri.

[XXIV] "CONCERNING THE UNIVERSE, THE CITY OF GOD"

Concerning the universe, the city of God,
we know very little.
It was cooked for a long time
over a low flame.

Now, according to some idiots,
things are speeding up,
an acceleration that seems almost
a prelude to total extinction.

Perhaps thought itself will survive
without the one doing the thinking.
What's left is sheer absurdity,
the black hole, the Encyclopedia
of zero.

[XXV] "AFTER THE INVENTION OF THE INTERNAL COMBUSTION ENGINE"

After the invention of the internal combustion engine
is life two or three times more worthwhile? It's a question
that nobody asks—*et pour cause.*

[XXVI] "WE'RE IMPRISONED IN AN ALLEGORY"

We're imprisoned in an allegory
to be deciphered by beings other than human.
Don't tell me, Clizia, that this is pessimism.
A rifle bullet doesn't know where it's aimed.

[XXVII] "PEOPLE TALK AND TALK MORE"

People talk and talk more
about black holes.

Io credo che il più nero
sia abitato da noi
e forse qualcuno di fuori
si chiede se dentro ci siano
bestie a due gambe o a quattro
o nessuna e nemmeno si parli
di piante e fiori.

[XXVIII] "SQUILLA IL TELEFONO"

Squilla il telefono
interurbano.
Che sia Giovanna?
Ci rivedremo
aveva detto magari fra trent'anni.

Ma ora mi pare che esageri.
Senza contare che sarà irriconoscibile
come me.

[XXVIX] "NEL CAMPO DELLA SCIENZA"

Nel campo della scienza
si fanno e si faranno
infinite scoperte e invenzioni.
Ma anche la pulce si rallegrò
quando trovò la pelle dell'uomo. Quale
mirabile veicolo di trasporto
di sangue a sangue.

I believe the blackest hole
is the one we inhabit,
and that maybe someone outside it
wonders if in here there exist
beasts with two legs or four
or no beasts at all, and that nobody
even mentions plants or flowers.

[XXVIII] "THE TELEPHONE RINGS"

The telephone rings
with a long-distance call.
It's Giovanna?
"We'll meet again,"
she'd said, "maybe in thirty years."

But by now I think it's too much.
Not to mention she must be unrecognizable
like me.

[XXVIX] "IN THE FIELD OF SCIENCE"

In the field of science
they're making and will keep making
infinite discoveries and inventions.
But even the flea rejoiced
to discover the skin of man. What
a marvelous vehicle for transport
from bloodstream to bloodstream!

[XXX] AL TELEFONO

Signore, conosco di quanto Ella [+++] il gregge. Eppure ascolti. Quando il tempo darà luogo al suo rovescio, non sarò io ma lei che passerà non senza indifferenza sulla mia pietra tombale. Così saremo pari. Non escludo l'ipotesi che delle due lapidi nessuno avrà notizia avendo il tempo deciso di sopprimersi. In tal caso il verdetto sarà di parità. Ma si dovranno aspettare milioni di miliardi di anni. A meno che il Creatore del Tempo abbia deciso di sopprimersi: ottima idea che farà imbestialire gli amici [+++].

[XXXI] "QUANDO ENTRO NEL CIMITERO"

Quando entro nel Cimitero
di S. Felice a Ema
debbo attraversare molte lapidi
e addirittura calpestare quella
di Enrico Nencioni
insigne letterato di cui conosco poco.
Non mi lusinga questo viaggio a due
mia cara pur sapendo che poche ossa
conservano di noi meno che nulla.
Resta quasi impossibile immaginare
la polvere di un duetto che non ebbe
nel melodramma della vita un posto di rilievo.
La parte mia, pazienza: non fu avara
di mentecatti o peggio; ma non priva
di un peso corporale. Ma la tua
quasi invisibile da chi non possedeva
i soli occhi che contano e che meno
vedono però distanze e strade.

[XXX] ON THE TELEPHONE

Sir, I know just how much she [*is one of*] the herd. But listen. When Time accomplishes its own inversion, it will be she, not I, who treads on my grave, and not without indifference. So we'll be even. I don't exclude the possibility that nobody will be aware of either of our tombstones once Time has decided to eliminate itself. In that case the judgment will be one of absolute parity. But we'll have to wait millions of billions of years. Unless the Creator of Time decides on self-elimination first: an excellent idea that could drive our [*pious*] friends crazy.

[XXXI] "WHEN I ENTER THE CEMETERY"

When I enter the cemetery
of San Felice a Ema
I have to go past many tombstones
and must actually walk across the grave
of Enrico Nencioni
a distinguished writer of whom I know little.
I don't hold out much hope for our voyage together
my dear, knowing as I do how a few bones
preserve less than nothing of what we are.
It remains almost impossible to imagine
our duet in dust having a prominence here
it never had in the melodrama of life.
My role is patience: a patience never eager
to suffer fools or worse, and yet not a role
deprived of bodily substance. But your part
is almost invisible to those without your eyes,
which are the only ones that count, even if less
able than others' to see distances and roads.

[XXXII] "LA TEMPESTA S'ANNUNZIA"

La tempesta s'annunzia
con radi goccioloni.

Sto davanti alla radio
in questa camera d'affitto.
Apro il Corriere pieno di morti
sono spese bene 250 lire.

Lampi e tuoni di fuori.
Domani leggeremo
l'entità del disastro.
Tutto quanto qui accade
appartiene al dominio
del verosimile.
Ma esiste davvero
il vero?

Qualcuno non un dio con barba
tenta di farcelo credere.
Ma il dio senza barba è
ben altro affare.
Non come appare a guardarlo
[+++] intendiamo.
Non [+++] ai fisici
fra [+++].

[XXXIII] "C'È CHI VIVE CON UN PIEDE DI LÀ"

C'è chi vive con un piede di là
e con un piede di qua.
Avevo sempre creduto che il Patròlogo
avesse scarsi rapporti con la vita terrena.
Meglio una commedia del Lasca? Mi sfuggivano

[XXXII] "THE STORM ANNOUNCES ITS ARRIVAL"

The storm announces its arrival
with a scattering of large raindrops.

I'm across from the radio
in this rented room.
I open *il Corriere*, full of fatalities
and costing a whole 250 *lire*.

Lightning and thunder outside.
Tomorrow we'll read about
the damage caused by the disaster.
Everything that happens here
belongs to the domain
of the apparently real.
But does it really exist,
reality?

Somebody, not a god with a beard,
is trying to make us believe in it.
The god without a beard, however,
is quite a different matter.
It isn't on the basis of appearance
[*that*] we comprehend him.
He doesn't [*show himself*] to physicists
among [*others*].

[XXXIII] "THERE ARE THOSE WHO LIVE WITH ONE FOOT THERE"

There are those who live with one foot there
and one foot here.
I had always believed that the Patrologist
had but slight connection to life on earth.
A Lasca comedy was preferable? Many words,

molte parole del vecchio gergo toscano,
non lui che in quell'acqua nuotava
come un pesce nell'acqua. Ed io sospeso
tra la vergogna di me e l'ammirazione per chi
gioca con i tempi come con la racchetta
un pallista ...

[XXXIV] "SI CREDE CHE OGNI AMORE SCACCI L'ALTRO"

Si crede che ogni amore scacci l'altro
senza tuttavia spingerlo nell'oblio.
La faccenda si complica così
e alla fine di tutto si è distrutti.

Distrutti in qualche modo, ma sempre vivi
senza surplus di disperazione.
Non se ne avvede che [+++] e dice
sempre in gamba, buffone!

Forse anche quell0 sta morendo in piedi.
Ma è difficile crederlo. Ognuno crede
di essere il solo vivente, il solo degno
del disegno di Dio in cui non crede.

[XXXV] IPOTESI

I grandi eruditi raccolgono
qualche briciola dello sfacelo universale.
Certamente le meno interessanti
e non tutti la spacciano per quel che vale
(il valore cioè di una formica).

E chi ha detto poi che un formicone
non sia un unicum come la dea Kalì?

slang in the old Tuscan dialect, escaped me
though not him, who swam in that stream
like a fish in water. And I was caught
between shame for myself and admiration
for someone who played among eras
like a tennis player wielding a racket.

[XXXIV] "THEY SAY EVERY NEW LOVE CANCELS THE OLD"

They say every new love cancels the old
though without driving it into oblivion.
In this way the affair grows complicated,
and when it's all over a lover's destroyed.

Destroyed in a way, and yet still alive
without any excess of despair.
The guy doesn't notice [*he's finished*], he says
he's still on his feet, the fool!

Perhaps he, too, is a walking corpse.
But that's hard to believe. Each of us believes
we're the only one living, the only one worthy
of God's plan in which we don't believe.

[XXXV] HYPOTHESIS

The great scholars assemble
a few bits of the cosmic collapse.
Certainly not the most interesting ones,
and not everyone offers them for what
they're worth (i.e. the value of an ant).

And anyway, who's to say that an anthill
is not a Unique Case like the goddess Kali?

E la macchina stessa dell'interesse
vale per quel che vale, cioè meno di se stessa.

[XXXVI] DOPO BENDANDI

Di giorno in giorno cresce l'importanza
del pianeta Giove.
Saremo declassati, inscritti d'ufficio
in serie B.
Più tardi in serie C D e così via.
Saremo ancora qualcosa ma può importare
a chi?

[XXXVII] "È QUASI CERTO CHE IL PIANETA GIOVE"

È quasi certo che il pianeta Giove
abbia qualcosa da dirci:
ma qui si preferisce farne a meno,
perché diranno piove sul bagnato
il calendario delle nostre disgrazie.

[XXXVIII] "LE GUERRE RELIGIOSE"

Le guerre religiose
furono inventate ad arte
per confondere le carte.

[XXXIX] "SE ANCHE SI SCOPRISSE"

Se anche si scoprisse
il come e il perché dell'universo
venire al mondo sarebbe
tempo perso.

And the machine looking after its interests
is worth what it's worth, i.e. less than itself.

[XXXVI] AFTER BENDANDI

Day by day the planet Jupiter
increases in importance.
We'll be downgraded, assigned by the office
to the B level squads.
After that, to the C, the D, and so on.
We'll still be something, but to whom
could it matter?

[XXXVII] "IT'S ALMOST CERTAIN THAT THE PLANET JUPITER"

It's almost certain that the planet Jupiter
has something to tell us:
but down here we prefer to do without it,
since to add that to our calendar of woe
would be called adding insult to injury.

[XXXVIII] "THE RELIGIOUS WARS"

The religious wars
were craftily invented
in order to confuse the issue.

[XXXIX] "EVEN IF ONE DISCOVERED"

Even if one discovered
the how and why of the universe
coming into this world would be
a waste of time.

[XL] "QUANDO LA SCIENZA AVRÀ ESAURITO"

Quando la Scienza avrà esaurito
i suoi mezzi di esplorazione
la moda volgerà verso San Espedito
ed altri santi di assai dubbia estrazione.
Campione di velocità sarà colui
che per più lungo tempo resterà seduto
il più famoso cantante sarà muto.

[XLI] "UN TUTTO CHE SIA IL NULLA"

Un tutto che sia il Nulla
ecco la meta delle scienze umane.
Un Tutto che sia un Tutto-Nulla.

[XLII] SIMON BOCCANEGRA

Mentre cantava il lacerato spirito
il basso fu inondato da diarrea.
Riuscì a occultarsi? Su questo la platea
restò divisa e il mondo biforcato
tra carne e Idea.

[XLIII] "MAI FU DIMOSTRATO CHE IL MONDO"

Mai fu dimostrato che il mondo
esiste e il come e il perché.
E così non sarà irrazionale
adorare la Dea Kalì.

Quando il Tutto e il Nulla coincideranno
come le 2 facce della medaglia

[XL] "WHEN SCIENCE HAS EXHAUSTED"

When Science has exhausted
all its means of exploration, it will
be fashionable to petition Saint Expeditus
and other saints of highly dubious pedigree.
The champion sprinter will be whoever
sits in the same place for longest,
the most famous singer will be mute.

[XLI] "AN EVERYTHING THAT MIGHT BE A NOTHING"

An Everything that might be a Nothing,
that's the object of Human Science.
An Everything that might be an Everything-Nothing.

[XLII] SIMON BOCCANEGRA

While singing of spiritual anguish
the bass was overcome by waves of diarrhea.
Did he succeed in hiding it? Concerning this
the audience was divided and the world split
between the flesh and the Idea.

[XLIII] "IT HAS NEVER BEEN PROVED THAT THE WORLD"

It has never been proved that the world
exists, nor the why and the how.
Thus it might not be irrational
to worship the goddess Kali.

When All and Nothing will come together
like the two sides of a coin

[XLIV] "GLI ULTIMI RIMASUGLI DELLA CREAZIONE"

Gli ultimi rimasugli della Creazione
di enorme quantità pensarono di rifondersi
e rendersi invisibili. Così il Creato
fin dall'inizio fu spaccato in due.
E così fu che il servo diventò padrone.
Invano i teologi hanno pensato
di rifondere in una le due [+++]
ma l'impresa fallì perché l'uno
detesta il 2 e ne è ricambiato.

[XLV] "NON C'È DUBBIO CHE SIA"

Non c'è dubbio che sia
alquanto macchinosa la teologia.

Pare assodato che lassù non siano
libri giornali e tipografie.

Inaudibile essere diversi
e uguali come guanto arrovesciato.

Un Nulla che sia il Tutto ecco un rebus
che lasceremo volentieri ad altri.

Domanda: era proprio necessario
venire al mondo? O non era meglio
starsene fuori?

La teologia supera di poche spanne
astrologia biologia e altre balle.
Perché qualcosa esiste?
Perché qualcosa non esiste?

[XLIV] "THE LAST DREGS OF MULTITUDINOUS"

The last dregs of multitudinous
Creation tried to melt themselves down
and be invisible again. Thus the Created
was split in two right from the start.
And thus the servant became the master.
Theologians have sought in vain
to recombine the two [parts] into one
but the attempt has failed because the first
detests the second and the feeling is mutual.

[XLV] "THERE'S NO DOUBT THEOLOGY"

There's no doubt Theology
is rather complicated.

It seems certain that up above
there are no books, papers, or printed matter.

An inaudible existence, different
and identical, like a glove turned inside-out.

A Nothing that might be Everything, a puzzle
we're happy to leave to others.

Question: was it really necessary
to come into this world? Wouldn't it be better
to keep clear of it?

Theology is a few inches ahead
of astrology, biology, and other nonsense.
Why does something exist?
Why does something not exist?

Esistono molti buchi o un buco solo.
Se dico *io* non dico una puzzonata?
Se dico io loro, non emulo Ridolini?

[XLVI] L'ART NOUVÔ

Si può essere celebri
bruciacchiando un asciugamano
con un accendisigari o con altro.
L'arte si fa gigante con la sua distruzione,
una gettata di zabaione cada
per caso sulla tela e il colpo è fatto.
Non sono invenzioni da ridere, sono le sole
che dicano la verità.
Ma quale?
Hanno diritto di vivere
come uomini o altri animali
P.S. E c'è ben poco da ridere.
Sono stato bravo anch'io.

[XLVII] "CHE L'ESSERE ABBIA SOVENTE INCONTRI E SCAMBI"

Che l'Essere abbia sovente incontri e scambi
con noi uomini
non implica parentela e in qualche modo
identità.
Tanto meno è uno specchio sfaccettato
che rifletta il destino parcellare
di ciascuno di noi.
È a noi vicino e da noi lontano.
Quando del tutto sfugge alla spettrografia
siamo perduti. Non è più possibile
il recupero.

Are there many holes, or one hole only?
If I say the word "I," aren't I talking garbage?
If I say "I/they," aren't I laughable as Ridolini?

[XLVI] THE NEW ART

One can become a celebrity
by scorching a hand-towel
with a cigarette-lighter or some such.
Art proclaims its genius by destroying itself,
a handful of zabaglione tossed
at random on a canvas and the job is finished.
These aren't laughable creations, they're the only
ones telling the truth.
But which one?
They have a right to exist
like humans or other animals.
P.S.–And very little deserves laughter.
I did a pretty good job myself.

[XLVII] "THAT THE BEING HAS MANY ENCOUNTERS AND INTERACTIONS"

That the Being has many encounters and interactions
with us humans
does not imply familial relationship or some sort
of likeness.
Much less is it a many-faceted mirror
that reflects the individual destiny
of each one of us.
It is near to us and distant from us.
When it goes entirely undetected by spectrography
we're lost. Recovery
is no longer possible.

[XLVIII] "NELLA VERANDA"

Nella veranda
mollemente allungata su la sedia a sdraio
tu scrutavi il pensiero di San Bonaventura
e altri giganti celebri e obsoleti.
Più tardi fosti accolta da un mondo eslege,
io nelle fauci della burocrazia.
Ma che importa? L'amore non si spezza
che col disprezzo e questo non albergò mai.

[XLIX] "L'IDEA CHE QUALCOSA ESISTA"

L'idea che qualcosa esista
in sé non per sé
può nascere soltanto nella zucca
d'un abitante di manicomi.

[L] "INCONTESTABILMENTE"

Incontestabilmente
alcunché deve esistere.

Ma a [+++] di questo
scienza filosofia teologia rossa o nera
fanno cilecca.

Se questa non è fede
uomini dell'altare o del microscopio
andate a farvi f.

(Postilla. Credo che tale
sia il loro punto d'arrivo.
Non è a questo che aspiro
io che qui scrivo).

[XLVIII] "ON THE VERANDA"

On the veranda,
stretched out at ease on the chaise longue,
you scrutinized the work of Saint Bonaventure
and other of the greats, famous and obsolete.
Later, you were welcomed by a world without rules,
I by the jaws of bureaucracy.
But what matter? Love isn't destroyed except
by disdain, and that never had lodging in ours.

[XLIX] "THE IDEA THAT SOMETHING MIGHT EXIST"

The idea that something might exist
in sé and not *per sé*
could have origin only in the melon
of an inhabitant of a madhouse.

[L] "UNARGUABLY"

Unarguably
something must exist.

But with [*regard to*] this,
science, philosophy, theology (red or black)
have all misfired.

If this isn't faith,
O men of the altar or the microscope,
then go f. yourselves.

(Footnote. I believe such
will be the point they arrive at,
and it isn't to that I aspire,
I who write these words.)

[LI] "È QUASI CERTO CHE ESISTANO"

È quasi certo che esistano
animali verticali
chiamati uomini
senza dei quali
la parola esistenza
non sarebbe mai sorta.
Questa certezza però
è incrinata da molti dubbi
ai quali si risponde
cogito dunque sono.
Forte [+++], ma non direi certezza.

[LII] "UNA ZUFFA DI GAS"

Una zuffa di gas
e fu l'avvento
del pallottoliere universale.
Ma chi aveva inventato
spazio e tempo?

[LIII] "IL PAPA POLACCO"

Il papa Polacco
giudica e manda per procura.
Perbacco,
così si è messo sul sicuro.

[LIV] "AVER SENTITO CANTARE"

Aver sentito cantare
i galli in Corsica
voleva dire essersi inoltrato
molto lontano in alto mare.

[LI] "IT'S ALMOST CERTAIN THAT THERE EXIST"

It's almost certain that there exist
erect animals
called humans
without which
the word "existence"
would never have arisen.
This certainty, however,
is fissured by many doubts,
to which one responds
I think therefore I am.
A strong [*possibility*], but I wouldn't say a certainty.

[LII] "A PUFF OF GAS"

A puff of gas
and that was the beginning
of the universal abacus?
But then who invented
space and time?

[LIII] "THE POLISH POPE"

The Polish Pope
adjudicates and calls for prosecution.
By Jove,
that's the way keep himself safe.

[LIV] "TO HAVE HEARD THE ROOSTERS"

To have heard the roosters
crow in Corsica
used to mean having ventured so far
as to be a long way out in the open sea.

Solo da due o tre vegliardi
udii parlare di simile imprudenza.
Era ciò che dai nostri mistici d'oggi
sarebbe detta la Transcendenza

[LV] SCIENZIATI TEDESCHI

Scienziati tedeschi appostati
hanno scoperto che all'aquila
basta un colpo di becco per decapitare
l'adultera.

[LVI] A TEMPO PERSO

Se un'esplosione ha prodotto
l'universo,
non potrebbe un altro botto
disgregarlo?

Once I heard talk of such rash behavior
from just a few elderly gentlemen.
It was what our mystics nowadays
would call Transcendence

[LV] GERMAN SCIENTISTS

Observant German scientists
have discovered that all an eagle
needs is a slash of its beak to decapitate
the adulteress.

[LVI] IN SOMEONE'S SPARE TIME

If an explosion produced
the universe,
might not another bang
undo it?

Notes to the Translations

FROM *SATURA*

"Satura," Latin for both "satire" and "variety show," was a classical genre adopted most prominently by Horace. Montale dedicated this book to *"Il Tu,"* that being the pronoun used in speaking to one's intimates, and it opens with two series of fourteen poems each (*Xenia I* and *Xenia II*) addressed in memory to Drusilla Tanzi (1885–1963), the poet's companion and ultimately his wife. *Satura* then has two more sections. Of the poems chosen here, "History" and "The Rhymes" belong to the first of these, the others to the second.

"Xenia I, 13"– The word *"xenia"* comes from the ancient Greek "hospitality" and means that which is due by custom and divine obligation to a stranger provided shelter. Drusilla Tanzi's brother Silvio (1879–1909) was a minor composer and music critic. His suicide is mentioned by his niece Natalia Ginzburg in *Family Lexicon (Lessico famigliare)*.

"Xenia II, 5"– Drusilla Tanzi was exceptionally near-sighted.

"Xenia II, 14"– The flood of November 4th 1966 caused great destruction in Florence, where Montale had lived previously and still had material in storage. Charles Du Bos (1882–1939) was a French literary critic noted for his interest in English literature. Ezra Pound moved to Italy in 1924, and Montale stated in a newspaper article that the two met in 1925 (not 1927, as some sources say). Alain was the pen-name of Émile-Auguste Chartier (1868–1951), a philosopher and critic; his *Commentaires* on the poetry of Paul Valéry appeared in 1936. *Canti Orfici*, written by the futurist poet Dino Campana (1885–1932), was published in 1914.

"History"–The Latin phrase *Historia est magistra vitae*, from Cicero's *De Oratore*, means "history is life's teacher" and remains proverbial.

"The Rhymes"– The *dame di San Vincenzo* of Montale's original are a laical association of women who raise money for Catholic charities.

"Letter"– The "you" is Drusilla Tanzi. Ottorino Respighi (1879–1936), a composer appreciated mostly for his orchestral tone poems, also wrote operas. Luisa Tetrazzini (1871–1940) was a coloratura soprano of great international fame. Marcello Malpighi (1628–1694) was a biologist and physician who made significant discoveries about the composition of blood. Giovanni Martinelli (1885–1969) was a tenor acclaimed in the role of Ramerrez in Puccini's *La fanciulla del West*. Tullio Carminati (1894–1971) was a movie actor best known to English-speaking audiences for his performance in *Roman Holiday*. Concerning the odd liqueur, Montale explained that it contained a "Pasticca del Re Sole," a licorice-flavored cough lozenge, and that these lozenges at one time contained "meconium." Meconium is the first feces of a newborn child, but the word is also used in Italian to mean raw opium (presumably because of the color and consistency). *The Count of Luxembourg* is an operetta by Lehár.

"*Le Revenant*"– Again, the "you" is Tanzi. Montale identified the "underground magazine" as *La Liguria Illustrata*, edited by the Genovese teacher and journalist Amedeo Pescio (1880–1952) from 1913–1916. Clizia is the name the poet uses here and on many other occasions for Irma Brandeis. Brandeis (1905–1990) met Montale in Florence in 1933, and the two became intimate. She returned to her native America in 1938 and went on to be a Dante scholar and a professor at Bard College, but her memory was of great importance to Montale, and she figures often in his work. The original Clizia is a nymph transformed into a sunflower in Ovid's *Metamorphoses*, but

Montale stated in an article that his source for the symbolic name was its use for the beloved in a sonnet in *The Rhymes* of Dante. The speaker of that poem is faithfully lovelorn, and Montale calls this the typical situation of "every lyric poet who lives besieged by the absence/presence of a distant woman."

"The Arno at Rovezzano"– Rovezzano lies on the right bank of the Arno on the outskirts of Florence. "*Tu che fai l'addormentata*" is the Italian version of an aria Méphistophélès sings in Gounod's *Faust*; Montale received operatic training in his youth and had hoped to debut in this opera. The Judas-tree (*Cercis siliquastrum*) is a shrub with pink flowers popularly believed to be the tree from which Judas Iscariot hanged himself. Montale stated in a letter that this poem is addressed to "an abbess... by the name of Sister Jerome (previously called Baroness von Agel)." Baroness Melanie Olivia Julie von Nagel zu Aichberg (1908–2006) was a poet and translator who published as Muska Nagel. Born in Berlin, she lived in Florence between the wars, married the Dagestani portrait artist Halilbeg Mussayassul in Munich in 1944, and moved to America soon after. Following the death of her husband in 1949, she became a nun and eventually entered the Benedictine abbey of Regina Laudis in Bethlehem, Connecticut, under the name of Sister Jerome von Nagel Mussayassul.

"Down There"– In Italian culture, the juxtaposition of the sacred and the profane constitutes obscenity, so that associating divinity with a dog is deeply offensive rather than euphemistic. Thus, to search for saints among dogs implies insult and outrage in addition to squalor. *Flatus vocis*, meaning "weightless words" or "empty talk," is an expression attributed to Roscellino di Compiègne (d. ca. 1120), a nominalist theologian who held that philosophical concepts have no objective reality beyond the breath exhaled in pronouncing the terms used for them.

"Rebecca"– The episode of Rebecca at the well is found in chapter 24 of *Genesis*.

FROM *DIARY OF '71 AND '72 (DIARIO DEL '71 E DEL '72)*

Like *Satura* and indeed most of Montale's books, this volume is divided into sections, the first for poems composed in 1971 and the second for those of the following year. Of the eight poems I have chosen to translate here, the first five are taken from the 1971 section, the others from that of 1972.

"The *Arte Povera*"– By now internationally recognized, the *arte povera* was an aesthetically radical movement that originated in Italy in the late 1960s and employed non-traditional materials to create anti-establishment art. The *carta da zucchero* of Montale's Italian is the grayish-blue paper formerly used to package loaves of sugar; sugar is rarely sold that way now, but the distinctive color is still remembered. Sainte-Adresse is a seaside town in Normandy, now essentially part of Le Havre. Johan Jongkind (1819–1891) was a Dutch forerunner of Impressionism known for his coastal landscapes.

"Fire"– Via Bigli is a street in the center of Milan on which Montale lived for nearly three decades, first at number 11 and thereafter at number 15.

"The Clock with the Carillon Chimes"– *The Bells of Normandy* (*Les cloches de Corneville*) is an opera by Robert Planquette (1848–1903). The *libeccio* is a southwest wind that often blows hard in Liguria. The word *"toriada"* (a literary term for bullfighting ritual) in the original is Spanish rather than Italian, and the translator Gyan Shyam Singh (who was acquainted with Montale) believed it to be a reference to the poem of that name by Fernando Villalón (1881–1930).

"The New Iconographers"– *La legge Merlin* (the Merlin statute), named after the World War II partisan and subsequent Senator-for-Life Angelina Merlin, closed the brothels in Italy as of February 20, 1958. Giorgio Alvise Baffo (1694–1768) was the author of over twelve hundred poems in Venetian dialect, many of them salacious. The 1972 Olympics in Munich saw a terrorist attack in which eleven members of the Israeli delegation were killed, among others.

"Lake Sorapis, 40 Years Ago"– The Engadin Valley in Switzerland is where the expensive resort of St. Moritz is located. Lake Sorapis is in northeast Italy, near Cortina d'Ampezzo. Mosca, meaning "fly," was the nickname of Montale's wife Drusilla Tanzi, given to her because the thick lenses required to correct her myopia made for an insect-like appearance. *Hic manebimus optime* ("this is the best place for us to remain") is a phrase taken from Livy. The words, originally an asseveration of patriotic attachment to ancient Rome, were used by Gabriele D'Annunzio for nationalist purposes following World War I but are now most often referenced humorously.

FROM *FOUR-YEAR NOTEBOOK (QUADERNO DI QUATTRO ANNI)*

"Honor"– Guido Piovene (1907–1974) was a novelist, critic, and journalist born in the Veneto, a region Montale evidently considered more voluble than his own notoriously laconic Liguria. A Fascist in his youth, Piovene revised his politics following World War II. Cecco Beppe ("Freddy-Joe") was the Italian nickname of Franz Josef the First (1830–1916), the reactionary Austro-Hungarian Emperor during whose long reign (1848–1914) northern Italy freed itself from Austrian rule. Montale served in the Italian infantry during World War I and saw action in Vallarsa, an alpine valley north of Verona.

"Reading Cavafy"– Cavafy wrote two poems in which the Furies approach Nero, one called "The Eumenides' Footsteps" ("α β ματα των υμεν δων'") and a later revision called "The Footsteps" ("α β ματα").

"For a Cut Flower"– The Eurasian blackcap, *Silvia atricapilla*, is a small warbler whose range includes Italy. There is critical consensus that poems involving this bird refer to the woman Montale else-where calls Arletta or Annetta, a muse-like figure based on a friend of the poet's youth named Anna degli Uberti (1904–1959). Although she did not succumb to breast cancer until well into middle age, Montale always treats her as one who died tragically young.

"Soliloquy"– Richard Wagner and Henry James were each a frequent visitor to Venice. Wagner composed part of *Tristan and Isolde* there in the Palazzo Giustiniani during the winter of 1858–1859. San Gior-gio is the island in Venice which houses the Cini Foundation, a cul-tural center. The man to whom the future belongs cannot be Pier Paolo Pasolini, as this poem was written some eight months prior to his sensational murder in November of 1975. G. Singh's note on the subject states flatly that the reference is to the art historian J. J. Winkelmann (1717–1768), also killed in squalid circumstances. Win-kelmann, however, is hardly a man of the future and in any case lived mostly in Rome and is not associated with Venice.

"The blackcap wasn't killed"– Again, the blackcap is to be identified with Anna degli Uberti.

"Questions without an Answer"– The *canzoniere* of Montale's orig-inal refers in this context to Petrarch's cycle of love poems. "Onlie begetter" comes from the dedication of Shakespeare's sonnets. The *trobar clus* was a hermetic style practiced by some 12th and 13th century Occitan poets. That words are the consequences of things is an allusion to Dante's *La Vita Nuova* ("*Nomina sunt consequen-tia rerum*"), but the idea goes back to the *Institutes* of Justinian.

"Beside Lake Orta"– The closing lines here recall the words Pope Gregory the Great is said to have exclaimed upon seeing English children in a slave market: "*Non Angli, sed angeli, si forent Chris-tiani,*" i.e. "Not Anglos, but angels, if they were Christian."

"In a Northern City"– An early draft of this poem shows the city intended is Scandinavian. Note that the driver uses the Spanish word for democracy. Rafael Lasso de la Vega, Marqués de Villanova (1890–1959), was a Spanish poet who lived in Florence from 1942 to 1948 and was one of the authors who frequented the Le Giubbe Rosse café.

"Aspasia"– Aspasia (ca. 470 B.C.–410 B.C.) was a courtesan and the consort of Pericles, the leader of Athens in its Golden Age. Admired for her sagacity and the hostess of what we would now call a salon, Aspasia was one of the very few women in ancient Greece of known political influence. Perhaps predictably, she was accused by detractors of being a procuress and brothel keeper.

"Protect me"– Although he continued to appear in the *Grand Larousse encyclopédique*, the entry for Montale was dropped from the 1975 edition of the *Petit Larousse Illustré*. Evidently the omission still rankled at the time this poem was written in December of 1976.

"Lakeside Drive"– Campione is located in an Italian enclave within Switzerland on the east shore of Lake Lugano.

"Mirages"– Montale explained in an interview that the speaker of this challenging poem is to be imagined as peering through a keyhole at the first act of the Richard Strauss opera *Arabella*. The fortune-teller is dark in color due to her ethnicity, and the beer-soaked sot and latter-day Christian knight are to be understood as the composer and his librettist Hugo von Hofmannsthal respectively. Strauss had a reputation for imbibing. His mother was the heiress to a brewing fortune, and he drank the family product from an early age.

OTHER POEMS (ALTRI VERSI)

"…leafy cupolas from which a polyphony"– Tellaro is a Ligurian seaside town just south of Lerici, near the Gulf of La Spezia.

"The Fleas"– The reference is to John Donne's poem "The Flea." Montale shared an enthusiasm for Donne with Irma Brandeis, and he mentions their reading this poet together often in his work. In general, Montale's frequent allusions to Donne are accompanied by memories of Brandeis and carry an erotic charge.

"Prose for A.M."– Anne More, who died in childbirth in 1617, was the wife of John Donne. Montale was himself a widower at the time of this poem's composition, and while any reference in his poetry to Donne necessarily evokes the memory of Irma Brandeis, his theater companion here looks to be Tanzi. The "cacciucco" of the original is a fish stew typical of Tuscany and Montale's native Liguria.

"The Big Bang must have produced"– Once again, the blackcap is to be identified with Anna degli Uberti.

"Zigging and Zagging"– A *Kobold* (Italian *coboldo*) is an inimical subterranean gnome of Germanic folklore. The presumably German priest who is the *Kobold* in this poem might be Karl Rahner (1904–1984). A prominent Jesuit theologian, Rahner sought to blend transcendental Thomism with the philosophy of Kant and Heidegger, and he was appointed an advisor to the Second Vatican Council. The Ecumenical Council of Constance, held from 1414 to 1418, was notable in part for the condemnation of Jan Hus as a Protestant heretic. The English poet John Wilmot, Lord Rochester (1647–1680), a notorious libertine, was reported to have made a deathbed conversion to Anglican Christianity. His wife Elizabeth Malet, born in 1651, survived him by a year.

"Ruminating"– St. Bonaventure (ca. 1217–1274), a Father of the Roman Catholic Church and scholastic theologian, was noted for his attempts to reconcile diverse philosophical traditions. Here as elsewhere, C. stands for Clizia, i.e. Irma Brandeis. *Non possumus*, Latin for "we cannot," is a phrase used by several Popes in their refusal to subordinate ecclesiastical matters to civil authority.

"Today"– In Italian, "*Il ratto d'Europa*" can mean both "The Rape of Europa" and "The Rat of Europe," but in English one must choose. Regarding the "*punto perso*" of Montale's original, the proverb "*Per un punto Martin perse la cappa*" tells how a cleric lost preferment due to a small error overlooked in punctuating a notice.

"Nursery"– Written in 1819 by Émile Debreaux (1796–1831), "*En avant Fanfan-la-Tulipe*" is a rousing song about the adventures of a young innocent in the army. The poem's allusion to Horace and Wilfred Owen ("*dulce et decorum est...*") recalls the mass bloodshed of WWI.

"With what voluptuous delight"– The line "*Et tout le reste c'est du charabia*" ("And all the rest is gibberish") suggests an attack on the French literary critics whose theories were sweeping academia in the 1970s. A draft of the poem, however, speaks of the "masters of heaven" who "salvaged their cathedras." It is typical of Montale to mock clerics and professors simultaneously.

"It isn't cruel like Valéry's sparrow"– Paul Valéry's poem "*L'oiseau cruel*," appears in his collection *Pièces diverses de toute époque*.

"One may be on the right"– The meal Montale has chosen here is *buridda*, which, like the *cacciucco* of "Prose for A.M.," is a fish stew of his native Liguria.

"In the Orient"– Jesus' words in the *Gospel of Matthew*, that "It is easier for a camel to go through the eye of a needle than for a rich man to enter into the kingdom of God," are thought by some scholars to be the result of scribal error (others believe wordplay was intended). The term for a camel in Greek is very close to that for a rope, and the same is true in both Hebrew and Aramaic. Montale uses "string" (*spago*) rather than "rope" (*fune*), possibly for the rhyme.

"At First Light"– The figpecker is the popular name of the Orphean warbler (*Sylvia hortensis*). Its migratory range includes Italy, where in the summer months it is often seen in gardens, as its scientific name implies.

"Monologue"– Montale attended Genoa's Vittorino da Feltre Institute, run by the Barnabite Brothers, from age twelve to fifteen.

"To My Friend Pea"– Enrico Pea (1881–1958) was a novelist, poet, and theater producer. Leopoldo Fregioli (1867–1936) was an actor and quick-change artist. Sarzana is a town south of La Spezia where Pea lived for a while before dying of tuberculosis.

"Nixon in Rome"– President Nixon made a state visit to Europe soon after his inauguration in 1969. On March 2nd he flew from Paris to Rome, where met with Pope Paul VI, but he departed that evening without attending any festivities. Niccolò Jommelli (1714–1774) was a Neapolitan composer known for his innovations in the *opera seria* form. *Les Brigands* is a comic opera by Offenbach in which society is depicted as cheerfully amoral and the forces of order as both corrupt and incompetent.

"Càffaro"– Via Càffaro in Genoa is a steep street that climbs from the old city center up to the residential neighborhood of Castelletto. The journal *Il Càffaro* was founded by Anton Giulio Barrili in 1875, but during Montale's schoolboy years the senior editor was Pietro Guastavino. Càffaro di Rustico da Caschifellone (1080–ca. 1164) was a soldier, diplomat, and author whose *Annals* are primary source material for the history of medieval Genoa. The city paid to have the Latin originals translated into Italian. Flavio Andò (1851–1915) was a prominent actor who had toured with Eleanora Duse.

"At the Giardino D'Italia"– Valery Larbaud (1881–1957), the well-known novelist and poet, was a mentor and friend of Montale's with whom he conducted a correspondence. Il Giardino d'Italia was located in Genoa's Acquasola public park and existed from about 1870 until the early 1950s. A restaurant and café, it was a chic meeting place, as well as the site of outdoor dances, concerts and theater performances. Lothario and Mignon are characters from Larbaud's novel *Fermina Márquez*. A rum punch "all'italiana," or more often "alla livornese," is made using coffee rather than tea.

"Thirty years have passed, maybe forty"– The American scholar Charles Singleton (1901–1985) was a friend of Irma Brandeis and thereby of Montale's during the 1930s. He would later become famous as a translator of Dante, but as of 1936 he had already edited a collection called *Carnival Songs of the Renaissance (Canti carnascialeschi del Rinascimento)* and was knowledgeable regarding old Italian dialects. A Florentine chess club used to meet at the Caffè Le Giubbe Rosse.

"Succulents"– Cesare de Lollis (1863–1928) was a professor of literary history and taught for a time at the University of Genoa.

"Kid Duffer"– Palmaria is an island close to Porto Venere at the mouth of the Gulf of La Spezia.

"Hiding Places II"– The solitary sparrow of line eleven alludes to Leopardi's "*Il passero solitario*," a poem in which a lone bird's unselfconscious existence is contrasted to the detached melancholy and morbid self-awareness of the poet. The soprano aria from Massenet's *Manon* that reminds Montale of birdsong could be the famous "*Adieu, notre petite table*," but it is probably a mistake to seek too closely here; an earlier poem ("Annetta," written in 1972) mentions a solitary sparrow whose song is reminiscent of a tenor aria in the same opera. Corniglia is a Ligurian coastal village that constitutes one of the Cinque Terre. Situated on a cliff, it is visible from Monterosso, the town in which the Montale family owned a home.

"October Blood"– Mesco Point (Punta del Mesco) is a promontory at the north end of the Cinque Terre and quite close to Monterosso. The area is known for its marble quarries.

"An Invitation to Lunch"– Montale was in Israel/Palestine in 1964 as a correspondent-at-large reporting on the visit to the Holy Land of Pope Paul VI. The Catholic nuns referred to are most likely the Franciscan Sisters of the Church of the Beatitudes, a community established in 1938 on a hill by the Sea of Galilee said to be the site of the Sermon on the Mount.

"In Doubt"– *Cacania* is Montale's Italianate spelling of the scatological name Robert Musil gave to the old Austro-Hungarian empire in his novel *A Man Without Qualities* (*Der Mann ohne Eigenschaften*). The Empire was known as *kaiserlich-königlich*, or KK, pronounced "caca," from which Musil derived *Kakania*.

"Glory or Something Like It"– The Rencontres Internationales de Genève is an organization promoting cross-disciplinary cultural studies that was founded in 1946. Despite what the poet says, it still exists. Afrikan Aleksandrovich Spir (1837–1890) was a Russian philosopher noted for his influence on Nietzsche; he moved late in life to Geneva and became a Swiss citizen. Mazara del Vallo is a town in western Sicily, Pamplona the well-known town in northern Spain.

"It seems impossible"– Drusilla Tanzi died on October 20th 1963 and was cremated.

"No more news"– Drusilla Tanzi was buried, as Montale himself was later, in the cemetery of San Felice a Ema, located on the southeast periphery of Florence.

"Wipe your misty eyeglasses"– As mentioned earlier, Drusilla Tanzi did not see well, and her eyeglasses had thick lenses. The big meal of the day for Italians is eaten at 1:00 PM, meaning that at noon dinner is soon to follow.

"My Swiss timepiece had the vice"– This is the first of eleven consecutive poems that concern Clizia/Irma Brandeis. Brandeis left Italy at the beginning of August 1938, going first to Croatia and then to France before returning to The United States in September. The café where Montale is saying goodbye to her, located in Piazza San

Marco in Florence, was known in the 1930s as a gathering place for those of anti-Fascist sympathies.

"Of Luni and Other Things"– Luni, Poveromo, and Fossa dell'Abate are situated on the west coast of Italy between La Spezia and Viareggio. Luni is the site of Etruscan ruins. An early draft of this poem makes it clear that the companion is Clizia/Brandeis, and that the *jeunesse dorée* are the Etruscan youths who must once have come to this shore for recreation. Gabriele D'Annunzio's collection of poems *Alcyone* (1903) was written in and treats of various locations in the area.

"Clizia Says"– The expert in both demotic sermons and patristic phrasing is Charles Singleton. See the note to "Thirty years have passed, maybe forty..."

"Internal/External"– The Pensione Annalena, south of the Arno on Via Romana, was where Irma Brandeis stayed in Florence. Giovanna Calastri (1913–1974), the daughter of the *pensione*'s owner, lived for much of her life in America, and she and Brandeis were good friends. Montale knew her as well, and when the poet visited the States briefly in 1950, he in fact met with Calastri but not Brandeis. Thus, the dimly remembered identity and unrecognizable voice in this poem are likely a fiction. The voyage referred to is not that of Brandeis' departure from Europe in 1938, but rather a passage from Genoa to New York that Calastri and Brandeis made together on the S.S. Rex in September of 1933.

"Quartet"– Camillo Sbarbaro (1888–1967), a native like Montale of Liguria, was a poet as well as a botanist specializing in mosses and lichens. Elena De Bosis Vivante (1905–1963) was a painter prominent among a group of artists and intellectuals centered in Siena. She and Sbarbaro carried on an extensive correspondence.

"Since life is fleeting"– In Italian, the letter "è" (if accented) is the third personal singular of the verb "to be" and is thus the letter of the alphabet that "renders existence possible."

"I Believe"– Via Benedetto Varchi 6 is situated on the north side of Florence, near Piazzale Donatello. From 1929–1939, Montale rented a room there in the home of Drusilla Tanzi (who would eventually marry the poet) and her then husband, the art critic Matteo Marangoni. Irma Brandeis taught at Bard College from 1944 until 1979. As Jonathan Galassi has pointed out, Bard is located in New York, not New Jersey.

"To Claudia Muzio"– The famous opera soprano died in 1936 at the age of 47. Her most acclaimed role was Violetta in *La Traviata*, and the penultimate line in this poem recalls that character's despairing outburst in the face of impending death: "*È tardi!*" ("It's too late!")

"When the blackcap"– As noted above, the blackcap is identified in Montale's poetry with Anna degli Uberti. This is then the first of five poems inspired by her memory that Montale placed at the end of his final individual volume and thus as a capstone to his work. Albert Savarus, the title character of a Balzac novel, is disappointed in love due to the malicious interference of a jealous woman.

"Beloved of the Gods"– "Those whom the gods love die young" is a saying that can be traced back to Menander. Anna degli Uberti in fact lived to age fifty-four, which is the import of the "*bien cinquante ans*" in the possibly misattributed quotation from Rousseau.

"A Visit"– Anna degli Uberti's family residence in Rome was at 7 Viale Pola. Montale's epigraph date of 1922 seems unambiguous, yet in *Complete Poems* the editor Giorgio Zampa assigns the poet's first visit to the city to 1923. The Fascist March on Rome that brought Mussolini to power took place in 1922, however, and a conjunction of private distress with public calamity may be intended, particularly since Anna's mother was of Jewish extraction. The Dragoni hotel—site of a later attempt to assassinate Mussolini—was in Piazza Colonna, across from the Palazzo Chigi. The *buccellati* of the original are soft, sugar-coated cookies filled with fig jam and traditionally eaten at Christmas; Cerasomma is a village just west of Lucca.

"A Note on 'A Visit'"– Following World War II, Marxist ideology became almost *de rigueur* in Italian academic and literary circles, and the notion of historical necessity became an intellectual orthodoxy. Montale was skeptical of this ideology. Cf. "History" in *Satura*.

"Ah!"– In 1922 Anna degli Uberti attended the Collège Les Tilleuls, a secondary school located in Annecy in southeastern France. In the original, the final line of the poem consists of the single syllable "Mah?" This untranslatable utterance is extremely common in Italian and is used to express a non-committal dubiety. Thus, the last word of the last volume Montale published in his lifetime constitutes a retreat into skepticism and inconclusion. This was certainly intentional, as the typescript carries the author's handwritten note *"forse il libro potrebbe finire con questa poesia"* ("perhaps the book could end with this poem").

FROM *FUGITIVE POEMS (POESIE DISPERSE)*

Montale's *The Work in Verse* of 1980 includes a section called *Fugitive Poems (Poesie disperse)*. This comprises seventy-eight poems composed at various stages of his career which were unpublished in book form previously but had appeared in magazines or been preserved in typescript. Of these, I have selected those written late in life that seem to me the most substantial.

"Little Diary"– Existing in two typescripts, dated February 2nd and 3rd, 1968.

"The Play"– Dated in typescript February 26th, 1969, this poem appeared in the Milanese newspaper *Corriere della Sera* on March 9th of that year.

"The Gift"– Dated in typescript April 16th, 1975.

"Empty Talk"– Dated in typescript June 12th, 1975. Riccardo Bruscagli identifies the quotation in line eight as an allusion to Petrarch's *Canzoniere* 128, line 94: "*fia il combatter corto*" (the struggle will be brief), which Machiavelli in turn uses in his conclusion to *The Prince*. Bruscagli suggests that perhaps Montale has misremembered or else has deliberately conflated his allusion with an echo of Dante's *Inferno* XXVII.110: "*lunga promessa con l'attender corto*" (a big promise with a small fulfillment). Certainly Dante is alluded to further on, as the lines "My protector left me by the wayside/out of some scruple of his own" evoke Virgil's sudden disappearance in Canto XXX of *Purgatorio*.

"The Glory of Useless Lives"– Dated in typescript February 13th, 1976. In an early draft of this poem, the *nom di guerre* mentioned in line nine is "Katzdfer." Perhaps a contraction of "*cazzo di ferro*," i.e. "iron-dick," this is the sort of alias that might have been used by a partisan during WWII. Margutte is a Gargantuan character in the poem *Morgante*, written in 1478 by Luigi Pulci (1432–1484). For *flatus vocis*, i.e. "weightless words," see the note on page 209 regarding "Down There."

"Life in Plain Words"– Dated in typescript October 20th, 1976. The title in Italian ("*La vita in prosa*") may be a punning reference to Edith Piaf's signature song, *La vie en rose*.

THE HOUSE IN OLGIATE AND OTHER POEMS (LA CASA DI OGLIATE E ALTRE POESIE)

Extracted from two notebooks Montale gave his housekeeper Gina Tiossi, who donated them to the library of the University of Pavia, this posthumous collection was assembled by Renzo Cremante, annotated by Gianfranca Lavezzi, and published by Mondadori in 2006. Almost all the poems in the Tiossi notebooks were written in the mid to late 1970s, the last years of the poet's life. An exception is "The House in Olgiate," which dates to 1963 and is composed in the oblique, so-called "hermetic" style of Montale's earlier work. Believing this poem to be the most important of the group, Cremante and Lavezzi used its title for the collection as a whole. In a few instances where the editors could not decipher Montale's handwriting, they left gaps in the text which they indicated with cross marks. I have kept these marks in the Italian, but in translating I have offered possible reconstructions within brackets. Much of this collection consists of material the poet would revise and reuse in the almost evolutionary process by which he composed verse, and some of the overlap with his other work is indicated in my commentary. The editors assigned each poem a roman numeral for ease of reference, and I have done as they.

[I] "The House in Olgiate"– This poem is of particular interest because it deals with a woman—Dora Zanini (1921–2009)—who seems to have functioned as yet another of Montale's many muses, but whose role as such has for the most part gone unrecognized. Zanini met Montale in Forte dei Marmi in the 1950s, when they were guests vacationing in the same hotel (the Albergo Alpemare). Like Montale at the time, Zanini lived in Milan, and she became close to him and his partner Drusilla, so much so that she sometimes served as their chauffeur and drove them about in her car. The occasion of this poem is a visit made to her onetime home in Olgiate, a town on the Olona river situated about twenty miles north of Milan. The house in question is the Villa de Ferneix, which has since been demolished, but which was located at 13 Via Roma, above an overpass that crosses the A8 *autostrada*. In 1939, at the age of eighteen, Dora Zanini married Piermario Tognella, eldest son of the family that owned the home, and their child Antonio–"Tonino"–was born the following year. Tonino died in a Florentine hospital in 1947, and the goldfinch that falls silent in the poem's third stanza is probably to be identified with him. The red lily whose shadow intrudes is the emblem of Florence, and although it is elsewhere one of Montale's symbols for Clizia/Brandeis, the shadow here seems to be that of the child's demise in a city Montale had once lived in but now left behind. The eyeglasses of the final stanza (which might typically refer to the myopic Drusilla Tanzi) likely belong to Zanini herself, who often wore the large dark glasses with tortoise-shell frames ("*tigrate*") that were fashionable in the 1960s. Hence she is a *tigre*, or tigress, thereby acquiring the sort of zoological nickname Montale often used for his muses. Zanini was originally from Trieste (as was Tanzi), and as a child she summered with relatives in the nearby Friuli village of San Giovanni di Casarsa. Unlike the other work in the Tiossi notebooks, this poem has appeared previously in English, translated by John Francis Phillimore in 2007.

[II] "I don't know if what I smell"– The poet's school-boy memory appears to be at fault, for Caligula, not Caracalla, is the Roman emperor said by Suetonius to have raised his horse to consular rank. Montale had been designated an Italian Senator-for-Life in June of 1967.

[III] "And now here come the herbicides"– The concern for a flea (rather than a weed) endangered by chemical threat suggests that Montale's memories of reading the poetry of John Donne together with Clizia/Brandeis are similarly faced with extinction.

[IV] "The Military Parade"– Montale mentioned in an interview that he had written a poem in which a figure representing Mario Tanassi, the Italian Minister of Defense on several occasions between 1970 to 1974, snaps to attention. Tanassi will figure again in "the days of the antelope were tormented..."

[V] "In the Apartment Block"– The episode of Esau and the dish of lentils is found in chapter 25 of *Genesis*. The stray feline turns up also in *Four-Year Notebook* in "About a Lost Cat."

[VIII] "They sent me a crown from Yugoslavia"– From Montale's correspondence it appears that he received an award from what is now Northern Macedonia in the autumn of 1975.

[X] "For having served his customers"– Da Bibe, Trattoria del Ponte all'Asse, is an old restaurant in the Galuzzo suburb of Florence. Bibe, the nickname of the original owner Paradiso Scarselli, first appeared in *The Occasions* in a poem called "Bibe at Ponte all'Asse." It should be said that the rat ragù, albeit clearly an offering consonant with the withering irony of late Montale, is the sort of dish for which some Florentine restaurants became known and even appreciated in the lean years of WWII and its aftermath.

[XI] "G. Pascoli"– Giovanni Pascoli (1855–1912) is among the most acclaimed Italian poets of the late nineteenth and early twentieth centuries. In her note to this poem, Lavezzi cites a newspaper article by Montale in which he objects to Pascoli's "disjunctions of tone," "absence of grand, memorable lines," and "constant formal and psychological wavering."

[XII] "Rarity of the Raptors"– An offspring of Minerva is found in a poem called "The Disappearance of Owls" ("Scomparsa delle strigi") in *Four-Year Notebook*. Cf. also the poem immediately following this one.

[XIV] "the days of the antelope were tormented"– This quatrain concerns the Lockheed kickback scandal that engrossed Italy in the late 1970s. The onetime Minister of Defense Mario Tanassi, who was convicted of bribery in March of 1979, had been referred to in company documents by the pseudonym "Antelope Cobbler."

[XVIa] "Life is like a cigar," [XVIb] "Like a Havana cigar," and [XVIc] "But if a cigar existed"– Cremante considered these three poems to be so similar in subject as to constitute drafts of one another, but felt that all three were worth printing.

[XVIII] "About-Face"– Montale had provided a version of this anecdote previously in an interview that appeared in *Playboy* in 1976. He saw Pound "a number of times from 1925 to 1935," but when they lunched is unknown.

[XX] "I'm walking chicken-hobble"– Cf. "Hiding Places II" in *Other Poems*.

[XXI] "We went over to the 'bow window' or some such"– This poem addressed to Clizia/Brandeis seems a first draft of "Predictions" in *Other Poems*, but the latter is dated in typescript a year earlier, possibly by mistake. Note that this version gives greater emphasis to the suggestion that Montale's treatment of Brandeis in his poetry is analogous to a lubricious raconteur's description of old conquests. The bay window, a feature of the Pensione Annalena, figures also in *Other Poems* in "Clizia Says."

[XXIII] "It's a mistake to believe"– Biffi Scala & Toula is a long-established restaurant in the center of Milan near the La Scala opera house. By the late 1970s, Montale had become internationally celebrated and his public appearances drew attention.

[XXVI] "We're imprisoned in an allegory"– The bullet ignorant of its target figures in other poems addressed to Clizia/Brandeis, such as "We went over to the 'bow window' or some such..." earlier in this collection and "Predictions" in *Other Poems*.

[XXVIII] "The telephone rings"– The phone call and Giovanna (Giovanna Calastri) appear at greater length in "Internal/External" in *Other Poems*. See the note to that poem.

[XXVIX] "In the field of science"– This poem may be compared to three others which were included in *Other Poems*: "Fleas," "Clizia Says," and "Since life is fleeting...". Here, too, the mention of a flea necessarily involves the memory of Irma Brandeis.

[XXX] "On the Telephone"– Immediately preceding a poem which addresses Montale's deceased wife Drusilla Tanzi, this piece clearly refers to her as well. If it was more than just a working outline, it is one of four Montale compositions that might be read as prose poems.

[XXXI] "When I enter the cemetery"– Montale's wife Drusilla Tanzi was buried in 1963 outside of Florence in the cemetery of San Felice a Ema, as was the poet himself eighteen years later. Enrico Nencioni (1837–1896) was a Florentine poet and critic and a translator of English literature. Tanzi and the cemetery plot appears also in "No more news..." in *Other Poems*, and her poor eyesight is the subject of Xenia II, 5 in *Satura*.

[XXXII] "The storm announces its arrival"– *Il Corriere della Sera*, one of Italy's major newspapers, raised its price from 200 to 250 *lire* in March of 1979. Gianfranca Lavezzi believes the scene of this poem to be a rented room in the Tuscan coastal town of Forte dei Marmi, where Montale summered that year.

[XXXIII] "There are those who live with one foot there"– The theater performance witnessed in this poem is found also in "Thirty years have passed..." in *Other Poems*, and here too the helpful scholar is Charles Singleton. Antonio Francesco Grazzini (1503–1584) was a Florentine apothecary, lexicographer, and literary partisan known as Il Lasca (a kind of fish proverbial for its vigor). Considered a master of prose, Il Lasca also wrote poetry and plays, and his comedy *The Witch* (*La Strega*) was staged in Florence in May of 1939.

[XXXV] "Hypothesis"– Montale used this title for two other poems, "Hypothesis" in *Four-Year Notebook* and "Hypothesis II" in *Other Poems*.

[XXXVI] "After Bendandi"– Lavezzi provides an extensive note to this poem, part of which I translate here: "On November 1st of 1979, the seismologist Raffaele Bendandi (born in Faenza in 1892) died; he was the author of an unusual theory—one ridiculed and contested by many scientists—concerning the cosmic causes of earthquakes and the solar influence on the human organism. In March of the same year, there was a major advance in our knowledge of the planet Jupiter, an advance made possible by the American space probe Voyager 1. Launched in 1977, the probe had arrived in proximity to that planet (reaching its nearest distance of 280,000 kilometers) and taken the first-ever up-close pictures of its atmosphere. Other photos and data were obtained the following month by the probe Voyager 2." Professional soccer leagues in Italy are designated A, B, C, and D according to the level of competition, and unsuccessful squads can be relegated to the league below. The planet Jupiter is visited again in the poem immediately following this one, as well as in "Jupiterian" in *Other Poems*.

[XL] "When Science has exhausted"– Saint Expeditus is said to have been martyred in Turkey in A.D. 303. He is traditionally the saint of just and urgent causes and is invoked for help with lawsuits.

[XLII] "Simon Boccanegra"– The Verdi opera is set in Montale's native Genoa, and the aria being sung is "*Il lacerato spirito del mesto genitore,*" which the poet once selected for an audition at the time he was considering a career as an operatic bass. It may be relevant that *Simon Boccanegra* was the opera performed for Adolf Hitler at Florence's Teatro Comunale during his visit in May of 1938.

[XLV] "There's no doubt Theology"– Ridolini was the stage name of the American actor Larry Semon (1889–1928). He was known for his slapstick silent comedy and was compared by many, including Montale, to Charlie Chaplin.

[XLVI] "The New Art"– Montale knew French well, and thus his title "*L'art nouvô*" is an ironic updating of *L'art nouveau*. In any case, he seems to be thinking of the abstract art that was new in the 1970s.

[XLVIII] "On the veranda"– This appears to be a draft of "Clizia in '34" in *Other Poems*. Clizia's reading of Saint Bonaventure figures also in "Ruminating," again in *Other Poems*. See the note to that poem. Brandeis' eventual return to America removed her from the social constraints of tradition-bound Europe, but it was also an escape from the anti-semitic legislation of Fascist Italy.

[XLIX] "The idea that something might exist"—*In sé* and *per sé* are translations of G.W.F. Hegel's *an sich* and *für sich*, which the philosopher uses to distinguish between an isolated, unreflective potentiality and an integrated, self-comprehending identity. Montale's dismissive attitude regarding this formulation was perhaps reinforced by his dislike of doctrinal Marxism, which was heavily influenced by Hegelian philosophy.

[L] "Unarguably"– Although black is a color associated with Fascism, given that this poem was composed several decades after the collapse of Fascist power, it seems likely that the phrase *"rosso o nero"* ("red or black") in the original describes the adherents of what Montale saw as the analogous dogmas of communism and Catholicism.

[LII] "A puff of gas"– This little poem exists in five very similar variants in the Tiossi notebook, of which Cremante chose to print this one as the most finished. The author's struggle with the idea explored in these lines itself forms the subject of "If the universe was born..." in *Other Poems*.

[LIII] "The Polish Pope"– Lavezzi suggests this poem was occasioned by the excommunication in 1979 of the Dominican theologian Jacques Pohier by Pope John Paul II (born Karol Wojtyla) and the condemnation for "errors of doctrine" of Pohier's book *Quand je dis Dieu* (*When I Say God*).

[LIV] "To have heard the roosters"– This poem and the one that follows, dated in manuscript "March 1980" and "1980" respectively, may be Montale's final compositions in verse.

[LV] "German Scientists"– Montale claimed to have seen a documentary in which an eagle killed its mate after having detected the scent on her of another male.

Index of Titles

DANTE ALIGHIERI The New Life
Translated by Dante Gabriel Rossetti; Preface by Michael Palmer

ANTONELLA ANEDDA Historiae
Translated by Patrizio Ceccagnoli and Susan Stewart

GUILLAUME APOLLINAIRE Zone: Selected Poems
Translated by Ron Padgett

AUSTERITY MEASURES The New Greek Poetry
Edited by Karen Van Dyck

SZILÁRD BORBÉLY In a Bucolic Land
Translated by Ottilie Mulzet

ANDRÉ BRETON AND PHILIPPE SOUPAULT The Magnetic Fields
Translated by Charlotte Mandel

AMIT CHAUDHURI Sweet Shop: New and Selected Poems, 1985–202

NAJWAN DARWISH Exhausted on the Cross
Translated by Kareem James Abu-Zeid; Foreword by Raúl Zurita

BENJAMIN FONDANE Cinepoems and Others
Edited by Leonard Schwartz

GLORIA GERVITZ Migrations: Poem, 1976–2020
Translated by Mark Schafer

ZUZANNA GINCZANKA Firebird
Translated by Alissa Valles

PERE GIMFERRER *Translated by Adrian Nathan West*

W. S. GRAHAM *Selected by Michael Hofmann*

SAKUTARŌ HAGIWARA Cat Town
Translated by Hiroaki Sato

MICHAEL HELLER Telescope: Selected Poems

RICHARD HOWARD RH ♥ HJ and Other American Writers
Introduction by Timothy Donnelly